END OF
INNOCENCE

TRULY|UNFORGOTTEN

END OF INNOCENCE

The untold stories behind the victims of child killer ROBERT BLACK

ZOË APOSTOLIDES

MARDLE

First published in 2022 by Mardle Books
15 Church Road
London, SW13 9HE
www.mardlebooks.com

Text © 2022 Zoë Apostolides

Paperback ISBN 9781914451454
eBook ISBN 9781914451713

A CIP catalogue record for this book is available from the British Library.

Every reasonable effort has been made to trace copyright-holders of
material reproduced in this book, but if any have been inadvertently
overlooked the publishers would be glad to hear from them.

Design and typesetting by Danny Lyle

Printed in the UK

10 9 8 7 6 5 4 3 2 1

Cover image: Shutterstock/Alamy

Dedicated to the victims – those
with names and those without

NB This book has been written based on facts,
interviews and testimony.
Some scenes have been created for effect.

PROLOGUE

This is a story about disappearances. A series of them – one the most well-publicised of its day. All those who vanished were female, all were children, all assumed murdered. It's a story that spans England, Scotland and Ireland between the mid 1960s and 1980s. It's a story about death and loss, despite no bodies having been found. But more than anything it's a story about victims – about why some narratives appear to matter more, while others are quickly forgotten.

The cases as a whole represented a seismic social change, the kind only brought about by moments of crisis. They raised questions about how crimes are reported, speculated on, how they twist and turn to fit the agenda of a particular reporter, newsreader or community.

This is also the story of many families – some well-known to the public, some unseen – and the horror they were forced to endure. What unites the first group of stories is their resolution, or lack of one. We can posit theories and suggestions, try to build something from the rubble left behind after the crimes, but without anything concrete it's impossible to bring about a firm ending for families, for detectives, for whole nations left reeling.

The hunt for who'd murdered the children would involve some of the most ground-breaking techniques in modern policing, change the course of detection and investigative co-operation, alter how the British public lived their lives, and ultimately how they allowed their children to live. The crimes were the first to be investigated under the command of a central officer, a "Supremo" responsible for cross-county co-operation; they were also the first to be linked via a computer system designed to increase efficiency and the ability to retrieve and cross-reference information easily.

For many years, the resolution of many crimes had been hampered by this lack of technology: a missing index card, illegible handwriting or a note dropped to the bottom of a filing cabinet could unwittingly assist a killer in their freedom and anonymity, enabling them to strike again.

Missing children make headline news. Splashed across the tabloids and broadsheets alike, they capture the public imagination. It might seem morbid, an unhealthy fascination – the sort of thing that ordinary, decent people simply don't want to read about. But our interest runs deep: in watching press conferences, reading news reports, understanding how all these pieces of the jigsaw come together to form a complete picture, we bring ourselves up close with the worst-case scenario. We can't shy away from it or pretend it doesn't happen. Instead, by engaging with such cases and under-standing how they came to be, we bring them under a sharp spotlight, the sort of brightness that allows hidden things to become visible.

Even those who claim to have no interest in missing people, in murder inquiries or criminal proceedings, cannot help but be touched by them. People wonder about where they were, what they were doing, on the night a crime took place. Implicitly, and perhaps subconsciously, they experience a sigh of relief – on this occasion, whatever else happened, they themselves escaped harm. There's no point pretending that life exists free of crime, and who knows how many of us have unwittingly been closer than we might think. The average person will, across the course of their life, walk past a murderer between 10 and 35 times.

While the media might have us think otherwise, a missing child is rare. Missing might mean many things: from lost, playing, hiding, at a friend's house or with a relative, to miscommunication, a game, an argument. Most missing children generally return home safe and well, unaware of the agony even 10 minutes of time-unaccounted-for can be for a parent. Many will relate to those heart-stopping moments in a supermarket, or at the beach, when, for seconds which seem to last a lifetime, they cannot see their child.

Every year around 70,000 missing-children reports are filed in England and Wales, more boys than girls. It sounds like a lot, but 90% are found within the first 48 hours. It's those who don't return home that make the headlines. Trauma is piled on trauma: first the loss of the child, the what-ifs and alternate realities, and then the full glare of a media hungry for details – a media that can also prove instrumental in whether

IX

or not the case is solved. Missing children sell newspapers: we know this. But not all missing children.

Publicity depends on all manner of things. In the cases detailed in the first part of this story there is no clear-cut, black-and-white answer. What's certain is that on the days in question, children with everything to live for left their homes never to return. No evidence of their running away was discovered, and they were not known to police beforehand. In some cases, they were simply too young to have got much further than 200 metres from home without some kind of intervention. Beyond this, though, everything is conjecture. We look for the most likely set of circumstances and work from there.

The importance of how much coverage a missing child receives is crucial. But who is afforded it? We know that the average low-income teenage boy who plays truant will receive a lot less press than a vanished middle-class girl at a private school. It's important to step back from the crime itself, sometimes, and look instead at the responses that crime elicits.

Due to the relatively recent nature of these crimes, many of the victims' families and friends continue to live their lives, each year taking them further from the point their grief and horror began, but also further from the hope of a resolution. Some scenes have been recreated or created for dramatic purposes. Out of respect, some details – particularly the most gruesome facts – have been omitted.

Storytelling is part of growing up. Children listen with rapt attention to tales of castles surrounded by deep, clear water;

princes and queens; trees higher than the eye can see; thick forests and trolls under bridges. They often want the same stories again and again, over and over. The really good ones, the satisfying ones, the funny or frightening or exciting ones.

As adults we turn to fiction for escape. The whodunnits, the crowded parlour rooms, the perpetrator paling as an investigator points a quivering finger: everything reassuringly tied up nicely. We expect order in our lives despite all evidence to the contrary. We want culprits caught, mysteries solved. We want the answers to questions, and we want them as soon as possible. If we can't change the fact that something awful happened, we want at least to know how, and when, and why.

But sometimes that's impossible.

Part One

"Please Drive Slowly Through The Village"

NORFOLK, 2010

It's not easy excavating a well, even less so in winter. It's January 2010 and no one wants to be here. Boots have crunched across snow to a spot in the field indicated by a local landowner. He's in his 70s now, an old man remembering something long buried, and perhaps irrelevant. But he felt impelled to call and, luckily, the Norfolk Constabulary have followed up. The four sergeants standing grouped around the excavation team rub their gloved hands together. This might be it. Unconsciously they're bracing themselves.

"How long d'you think it'll take?" asks one of the policemen.

"They could've brought something down to warm us up," says another. "One of those space heaters or a flask of tea."

The men are grouped round a ladder, thick and sturdy, its polished rungs unnaturally bright against the dull white of the snow.

"It'll take as long as it takes," says someone in a neon jacket, evidently in charge. "Depends how deep we're talking."

"Can't be too far down," says the first sergeant. "Else how'd he have seen it?"

"We don't *know* that he saw anything," says his colleague, quickly. "It was a long time ago."

The men with the ladder turn as one to the police, their interest piqued.

"What did you say it was about?"

"Missing girl," says the first sergeant shortly. "Cold case."

The men round the ladder seem to take a collective step back.

"No one told us that," one of them grumbles.

"Always the last to know," his friend agrees.

They move forward to the patch of ground indicated by the police. The snow's fallen differently here – a platform of whitish grey at a slightly higher level than that around it. Once the snow's been scraped and dusted off, the circle of raised ground is revealed to be a slab of concrete.

Now the drills can come out.

"Stand back," says the man with the largest drill, pulling goggles down over his eyes. The sound rips through the otherwise-silent countryside, a harsh, piercing snarl. As metal hits stone it becomes higher pitched, almost unbearably loud.

The police retreat to the stone walls that border the churchyard of St Andrew's. This will take a while. The war memorial stands on its own island of submerged grass, the arms of the crucifix weighted with compacted ice. Opposite they can see curtains being opened in one of the houses and a woman's face peering out, pale and watchful. They'd hoped to avoid the scrum of the village or, worse, media attention. That's why they've waited until now, 10am on a Monday

4

morning, when most people are at work and the kids are safely at school. In the distance the shriek of the drill continues. With any luck they'll be through soon enough.

The sergeants and constables haven't been told exactly what they're here for. They know the broad picture but not the details. They're required just to be present, to watch the engineers descend into the well and – potentially – be ready to seal off the scene. In the van there's a roll of fresh police tape, curled and waiting.

"When did they close it up, anyway?" says the youngest.

"No idea – must have been years ago. According to the Super, the bloke who rang in said something about the 80s."

"He's been sitting on it since then? Why the hell did he wait until now to tell us what he knew?"

"Not sure. He's old. Might've just remembered. It's probably nothing anyway."

"Well, fine, but what does he think he saw?"

"Black bags at the bottom of the well. It was in use back in the late 60s. If he needed a drink during the day he'd use the well, instead of going back to the farmhouse."

"And he saw these bags at the bottom after she vanished?"

"Apparently."

The drilling stops. They wait, expecting it to continue.

With the engineers changing position, clearing away first one area and then another, the noise has been consistent in its stop-start rhythm. Now it's silent.

"Reckon they've finished," says the sergeant. "Better take a look."

By the time they arrive back at the well, a small knot of people has gathered by the church doors. The younger ones crane their necks as the police cross to the disused well; the older ones know better, shooing them away down the path. They have a feeling what this is about, and for some of them the situation's complicated.

If they find nothing, word will reach the family – another false hope, another dead end. In some ways it'd be better that way. No use dredging up old pains, picking at scabs. But if there's something down there, it's only right that the parents and sisters should have their answer at last. If they do find something, that'll be that for the village of Metton.

Like so many other places – Hungerford, Hillsborough, Soham – Metton was, for a time, a byword for tragedy. The media never seemed to leave, not in the 60s or the 70s, and on every anniversary, and following every possible sighting. Will they really have to face all that again?

NORFOLK, 1969

The Easter weekend was exactly as they'd all hoped: dry, fine, sunny. The odd spell of wind, but that was normal for the east coast. As if overnight, everybody's gardens were abloom with flowers after the quiet grey of winter. On Easter Sunday, the church of St Andrew's had rung its bells joyfully for the 10 o'clock service. In the village of Metton, Norfolk, a tiny hamlet in eastern England, all was well.

Here the roads are narrow, bordered on both sides by high hedges of fullest green. Climb over the brush and bracken and you might trudge across lush fields and small brooks criss-crossing one another all the way to the city of Norwich, 30 kilometres to the south. In 1969, few cars passed through: some day-trippers nipping over from the nearby A140, a busy route following an old Roman road all the way up to Cromer and the chilly North Sea.

It's a typical coastal sort of place: calm, tranquil, the sort that in 20 years foreign tourists will write home about. Not yet, though. The war hasn't quite lost its grip on people: there's still a sense of waiting, of trepidation, of wondering when – not if – things will kick off again. After all, the second war wound its tendrils around the world just 20 years after the first. They're prepared for anything.

The council houses here are small and squat, cosy, well-kept. It's a cheerful-looking place. Boxes of geraniums spill over the edges of sills, tomato plants snake their way along pipes and the long round branches of trees tap the windows on the houses' second floors.

The front door of number three is open; it's always open. That's the way Olive likes it: bit of a breeze, even in winter. It's something the girls have always moaned about, or the older two at least. Never mind, she thinks to herself, finishing the ironing. She can do as she pleases now – Diane and Pamela have moved out, first one and then the other. At 20 and 18 respectively, neither lives very far away. At first it was tough, waving them off. But that's what having children's all about, isn't it? Preparing them, teaching them, guiding them, and then watching them leave.

Olive sighs. It's been a long day, always is in the week following Easter. Almost busier than Christmas, she thinks. Almost. The Fabbs – she and Ernest, her husband – are religious people, and Easter is the most important time in their calendar. They brought the girls up right, she reflects, folding the last of the tea towels. Although Diane used to moan about it, she always loved singing in the choir, Olive could tell. And Church provided a good community, a solid set of friends. Now they may have flown the nest but it doesn't matter – she saw them both over the weekend, for Mass and then for lunch. The smell of roast lamb and potatoes still hangs faintly in the air. It was a nice day. And April was so keen to help out, to ferry the gravy boats and dishes of vegetables, hot and steaming, back and forth from kitchen to table, chattering away, never ceasing for a minute.

April. Here she comes. A clatter of shoes on stairs, the fast pitter-patter of feet hitting wood. April. Their youngest, the only one left at home. Olive suspects she's been sad since Pamela left, since the place has gradually quietened with the departure of first one sister, then the other. In two weeks' time she'll be 14.

"I'm going to Roughton," she says, hopping the last steps into the kitchen, dipping her hand into the biscuit tin and pulling on her shoes seemingly all in one movement. They're new, these shoes – a much longed-for pair of wooden-soled sandals, and at last the weather seems fine enough, this past week, to wear them.

"Going to see Pam?" asks Olive. Pamela lives in Roughton, a village just a mile down the road.

"Yep, going to drop off a present," April replies.

She's a sweet kid, Olive thinks. It's Pam's husband's birthday and Olive knows she will want to offer him something, however small. She's been keen to feel a part of the grown-up gang.

"What've you got him?"

"Just some cigarettes," April says. A grown-up present indeed. "Players Weights. I'll take my bike. Won't be long."

"Take a jumper," her mother calls, as April makes to leave. The bike's parked just outside, in the garage, like it always is. It's April's proudest possession.

"No need, it's too warm."

"A jumper, April," says Olive sternly. Sometimes it feels as though she oughtn't to mother her so much, but she's not an adult yet – still just 13, after all. It's fair enough to ask your child to take a jumper on her bike ride, even if she won't be gone an hour. April has more than enough freedom and she's a sensible girl, but Olive isn't about to let her off today. She's putting her foot down.

"Fine," her daughter huffs. She trudges back upstairs and returns with a green sweater. "See you in a bit."

"Cycle carefully please," says Olive. She watches as April wheels the bicycle to the front garden gate and closes it slowly behind her. Her saddlebag, Olive can see, holds a single handkerchief wrapping the treasured, oh-so-grown-up present for Pam's husband.

"Tell them I'll be over later," Olive calls, and April nods. Nothing can keep Olive away from her grandchild for long. Another bonus to them living so close.

"Cheerio," she calls over her shoulder.

And now she's off, pedalling slowly down the road. The burgundy skirt, the green jumper, long white socks and the sandals – bright red with brass buckles. The blue and white bike. She's a picture in "Technicolor", a bright and rainbow-like thing. She's so grown up now and yet – Olive thinks, sighing, as she returns to the ironing – she's not quite there yet. Her doll still sits in pride of place on the mantelpiece, and April takes it to sleep with her each night. She probably wouldn't want her friends to know that.

The sun appears from behind a cloud and Olive feels relieved. She never likes to think of the girls out there in the rain, even if the journey's just a short one. April insists on taking her bike for everything – too much energy for her own good.

She thinks about what she needs to do before this evening, when Ernest gets home – he's been working long hours at the local construction firm, H Bullen and Sons. He earns good money, all of which he ploughs back into the family. Not a drinker, her Ernest, or a gambler. He simply earns his way and makes sure they're all looked after. A decent man. They've lived in Metton together almost 20 years now, raised their family here. It's been good to them. Their row of houses feels almost mansion-like, too, on its own private little road surrounded by tall trees and green fields. A perfect, safe playground for the girls.

She imagines April coming to the end of the gravel drive, probably cursing at the stones that threaten to unbalance her, and turning left. She'll be at Roughton in no time, travelling along the narrow Cromer Road until it forks along to Metton and the next village. Olive smiles as she thinks of her daughter free-wheeling, legs out on the slight downward inclines, excited to see her sister. Tonight, Olive thinks, she must remember to ask April what she'd like for her own birthday.

The day continues to be warm, unseasonably so. Olive finishes the ironing and starts on dinner, absently stirring a pan of mince and onions, chopping a carrot, adding a tin of tomatoes, tidying up and letting the sauce simmer on the stove. She sweeps the kitchen clean and starts on the

11

bathroom, making a mental note to ask April to please hang the towels properly or they'll never dry. She's surprised to note, coming back downstairs to stir the stew, that it's 3pm already. Funny how time flies.

The hours tick by and at 8pm, Olive wonders exactly how much longer April plans to stay out. She knows the rules and has never even tried to break them before, so Olive is sure she'll be home by 8.30, the absolute limit. She's cutting it fine, but why not? These are the school holidays, why shouldn't she stay with her big sister a little later? Olive just hopes that she doesn't leave it too much longer – that bike of hers has no lights. What's more, April loathes the dark.

At 8.45 there's still no sign. That's it. Annoyed, Olive pulls her own bicycle from the garage, closes the front door and sets off for Roughton herself. It's not a long journey but it feels like one today, for some reason.

There's no sign of April's bike outside Pam's house. Frowning, Olive pushes open the door and is greeted by the happy sight of Pam on the sofa, finally putting her feet up after a long day's work.

"Hello, Mum," says her middle daughter, rising. "Tea?"

"In a moment, love." She strains her ears for the sound of April's voice.

"Where's April?" she calls to Pam's back, as her daughter walks into the kitchen.

"April?"

"Yes, isn't she here? What time did she leave?" Olive must have missed her on the route home. April often takes the quieter path, Back Lane, off Cromer Road, especially if she has a bit of money to spend on sweets. Now Olive thinks about it, her youngest probably did have a little pocket money left over from the weekend. They must have passed one another, heading in opposite directions on different roads.

"Leave?" Pam puts her head round the door of the kitchen; her face has an odd expression, half bemused, half worried.

"Mum, she hasn't been here all day."

By 10pm that night, Olive and Ernest have exhausted all possible solutions for April's failure to arrive at her sister's. Ernest has been to the rectory, called on April's friends and asked neighbours to keep a lookout. At 10pm, admitting defeat, they ring the police.

"She set off for her sister's after lunch," Olive hears her husband explaining. "She should have arrived within 20 minutes." There's a pause. "Yes, sir, she's 13." Another pause. "No, not on foot. She took her bike."

Olive sits outside the phone booth with her head in her hands. Her emotions are jumping around – on one level she wants to shout at April, to scold her, ban her from going to Norwich tomorrow. How dare she worry them like this? On the other, a terrible fear – something she has never felt before in her life – is gnawing at her stomach, a sense of foreboding, an ache.

She realises her husband has finished the call. There's a silence. She glances up at the clear glass of the booth and sees him leaning his forehead on the wall above the receiver.

Her pulse quickens uncomfortably. He turns to look at her. "They found her bike," he says, in a choked voice. "Someone brought it in at 3pm. It was in a field just past Harrison's."

According to friends and family, April was a caring but shy girl, a regular babysitter, sensible. She enjoyed cycling, attended church with her parents, adored animals, made her own clothes. She had planned to go to Norwich on 9th April with a couple of friends. Most of the houses in Metton didn't yet have land lines, so she arranged the trip via a nearby phone box. She then had lunch with her mother and collected five pence ha'penny from the dining table before leaving the house at around half past one.

Shortly after, mere yards from home, April stopped to speak to some friends at Harrison's farm, on Cromer Road, in what was known locally as the donkey field.

"Look at this," she said, pointing to the basket.

The friends craned their necks to see, then grinned. "Cigarettes!"

April nodded. "They're a gift – I'm taking them over to my sister's."

"She wouldn't mind us having one... just the one. Go on April, be a sport."

April shook her head. "Look, I've got to dash. I'll stop in on the ride home, ok?"

They waved. "See you then."

Just after 2pm Mr Harrison – a local farmer – drove past the teenager on her bicycle, headed in the direction of

Roughton. Less than 15 minutes later, Ordnance Survey workers spotted a blue and white bicycle lying in a field beside the road. By 3pm, a local man driving his mother home also spotted the bike and, thinking it strange, took it to the Police House at Roughton. Officers on duty found the cigarettes, handkerchief and money still nestled inside the saddlebag.

April was born in 1955, but her story – such as the world knew it – began on the day she went out with a birthday present and never came home. How it ends still remains to be seen: April would now be in her 60s had life continued along the path she, her parents and sisters had all hoped.

There's no ideal time to go missing, but an isolated country lane in 1969 might be one of the worst. April Fabb never arrived at her sister's house on that sunny spring afternoon, and she has never been seen or heard from since.

There is no word in the English language to describe a parent who loses a child; still less for a parent who must endure the anguish of not knowing whether that child is in fact gone forever. When a 13-year-old goes missing, there is of course the possibility that the disappearance is deliberate, that the person doesn't want to be found, and that they were – somehow – savvy enough to set up a new life for themselves miles from home, to remain hidden while others searched.

April's disappearance constituted one of the largest investigations ever conducted by the Norfolk Constabulary, but it remains a mystery to this day. Over 2,000 statements were taken at the time; fields and waterways were scoured and drained.

On Thursday April 10th, 1969, the *Coventry Evening Telegraph* reported that police were "anxious to trace any passengers who travelled on the 3.38pm Cromer to North Walsham train on Tuesday" – they were clearly investigating the possibility, however slim, that April had left of her own accord. No one had seen her at any of the train stations she could have reached alone – and without her bicycle – on the day in question. Nobody came forward saying they'd noticed a girl fitting April's description either waiting for or onboard a train. But the possibility of a 13-year-old running away, however happy she might have been, couldn't be discounted. The ubiquity of her photograph, however, and police calls for the public to remain alert for April, made the lack of any sighting even more unsettling.

How could she just vanish?

It's a question asked time and again through the decades since. Newspapers wrote of the tracker dogs, the civilians trudging the deserted meadows, the hours of calling, searching, stooping to check the smallest piece of litter, the tiniest flash of colour in a hedgerow. Fingertip searches were undertaken while, above ground, an RAF helicopter scoured the area immediately surrounding the bicycle's discovery.

So what of the bike, the only piece of evidence recovered? It was undamaged, well cared-for, with no signs of a collision, though the bell on the handlebars was bent. This was likely to have occurred when it was thrown from the road into the field – presumably by a person of decent physical strength. It couldn't have been rolled down the bank. A traffic accident was ruled out, then. Robbery, too. Clearly the saddlebag was of no interest to whoever knew what had happened to April. A solitary fingerprint was recovered from the handlebars; when this was compared to items belonging to April at home, it matched.

For weeks her disappearance made headline news, both locally and nationally. And then, as these things tend to, and especially with no new leads, the case began to slip out of the public consciousness. Stories about April – along with possible sightings, speculation and theories – began to fade. Nothing more has since been found to shed the merest sliver of light on her disappearance.

A Dutch clairvoyant was even drafted in to try to shed light on the case. The use of such methods – telepathy, numerology and psychic readings – have long been controversial among most members of the policing community, not to mention outside it. Gerard Croiset was one of the exceptions to this rule. Born in the Netherlands in 1909, he trained as a watchmaker and then worked as a greengrocer; it was during this time that he declared his ability to discern major events in a person's life based on contact with a personal object. He set up a healing clinic with the aim of using his psychic gifts to help others, and by the end of World War Two had established a decent name for himself.

Scientists conducted a series of tests on Croiset's abilities, and were impressed enough to endorse him. It was then that Dutch police began to consult him for help in some of their most serious missing people or murder cases. In 1966, Croiset was involved in one of the biggest international manhunts in history after three children, Jane, Arnna and Grant Beaumont, aged between nine and four – disappeared off a beach near Adelaide on Australia Day. Croiset would be called upon again a decade later in the hunt for another child, the most high-profile of all his cases – and one that bore a striking similarity to what had happened in Metton. His advice proved fruitless, but his very inclusion shows just how far police were willing to go.

Years later, in 1997, the RAF deployed specialist thermal-imaging cameras to scour the ground for any disturbances near to where April's bike was found. Nothing. In 2010, a team of forensic anthropologists began using GIS mapping technology to assist in identifying the location of human remains. And in the same year, the old well by the village church was excavated – just on the off chance a local man's recollection might hold the key. All results came to nothing.

What seems most likely is that wherever April Fabb is now, she's not in Metton. It's probable that whoever snatched her from the street in broad daylight did not plan the crime. It was opportunistic, random, for how could they have guessed or arranged a kidnap based on the whimsical holiday plans of a 13-year-old? Whoever seized her, in the space of less than 10 minutes, was not only disturbingly daring but cunning too. They made sure to take her from her local surroundings immediately, and whatever happened next, they ensured she was never found.

April's father, Ernest, died in 1998; her mother, Olive, in 2013; both are buried at St Andrew's in Metton. Their wait for news was a long, agonising and ultimately futile one: they never stopped hoping, never stopped remembering their missing child. They had appealed to April directly through the press three days after she'd disappeared, a call that never received any reply. For some time after she'd vanished they refused to lock the front door, and left a light on in the porch. Now that her parents have gone, it is April's sisters who continue to hope for some news that might bring them closure.

St Andrew's in Metton was April's place of worship and that of her parents. It's likely she had many happy memories inside the building, meeting friends, going to Sunday school. The Easter weekend that marked her disappearance was the last time she would walk through its doors – probably in her best clothes, her favourite dress.

Beside the door of St Andrew's stands a memorial stone. Its inscription bears the words:

Will you of your charity remember in your prayers
April Fabb, a child who disappeared
from this parish in April 1969,
Of whom nothing
Has since been heard.

At each anniversary of April's disappearance, it's covered in daffodils.

SCUNTHORPE, 1973

The town of Scunthorpe had a population of 850,000 in 1973, when it formed part of the county of Lincolnshire. It was and remains a predominantly industrial place, the UK's largest producer of steel. Since 1996, following a county reshuffle, it's fallen under the umbrella of North Lincolnshire. For many years, it's had one of the worst child-poverty rates in the country.

For the inhabitants of Robinson Close, in the town's north west, things are especially hard. There's little money for the Space Hoppers and Raleigh Choppers which characterised the 70s, the Curly Wurly chocolate bars or *Bagpuss* toys.

Margery Markham wishes she could afford such things, but perhaps their absence makes the kids resourceful – determined to enjoy themselves come what may. She and her husband, Sidney, had done what they could before Sid left. There are just so many mouths to feed, always so much to do. And now she's doing it all on her own.

She can't believe how long the children take to get ready for school. It seems incredible, the amount of faffing before they're finally out the door. They should be able to fend for themselves a little more than they do, she thinks. Instead they need constant reminders: of gym bags, pencils, rubbers, rulers. They'd lose their heads if they weren't attached to their bodies. Her eldest boy, Graham, left school last year, and Carol's due to finish in a couple of months. He's still living at home, Graham, but at least he's working.

It's May 21st, pleasant and warm. They can make it on time if they leave now. Mrs Markham has to head to work herself: there's no use explaining to the foreman at the factory that the kids have delayed her. He won't have much sympathy with that.

Just last week she arrived 10 minutes after the shift had begun. He'd been waiting in the doorway, watching as she dashed across the forecourt, her handbag bobbing against her legs. She'd apologised before he'd even opened his mouth. It was the kids, she said. Bloody dithering like they always do. So much to sort out each morning, from breakfast to teeth cleaning and finding clean bits of uniform. Privately, she thought it a miracle she was there at all.

"It's not like they're young anymore, Mrs Markham," said her boss. And he's right, really. He's known their family for many years, for as long as she's worked for him, from back when they actually *were* small. Graham, Carol, Susan, Wayne, Christine and Melanie. "How old's your youngest now anyway?"

"Six," Mrs Markham sighed.

"Old enough to be getting himself to school, that lad, I'd reckon?"

"She. The youngest, I mean. Melanie."

But the man had already turned away, looking to the doors as the next poor soul trundled in late.

They are more than capable of getting themselves ready: Susan's 13 for heaven's sake. Wayne at 10 has a little more leeway. Today, only Christine can do very little wrong. She's still on a high from yesterday's celebrations for her ninth birthday.

None of them likes school. Mrs Markham doesn't blame them – after all, she didn't much like it herself.

At half past eight, the front door closes. She surveys her children, squabbling in front of her. Wayne has pulled Susan's hairband off her head and thrown it into next door's bushes. Susan's about to launch herself at him but their mother gets in the way.

"Go and fetch it," she says, in a voice that offers no room for manoeuvre. Wayne climbs over next door's gate and starts trudging slowly towards the bush. "Right now," his mother calls.

Christine is laughing, but trying not to show it. She and Susan have a special bond, but even Mrs Markham has to admit that right now her middle daughter has a face like a slapped behind; comical in its expression of deepest outrage.

"Right," Mrs Markham says, straightening Wayne's tie as he returns. "I'll see you later."

"What's for tea?" asks Christine. She looks at her mother intently.

"Same as usual, I bet," says Susan, still scowling. "Bangers and bloody mash."

"We'll have none of that," says Mrs Markham. "I'm doing my best, Susan, just you keep that in mind."

Susan looks briefly mollified before Wayne digs her in the ribs and the pair of them run off, shrieking.

Mrs Markham closes her eyes briefly against the shrillness before opening them and seeing Christine standing, ever so interested, before her.

"What's for tea?"

Mrs Markham sighs. "We'll go to the chippie if you like? Or I can pick something else up on the way home. Whatever you want, lovie."

How was she going to make good on that, she wonders, mentally counting the coins in the cupboard's almost-empty biscuit tin. There might be enough – just. Perhaps she can ask the foreman for next week's wages in advance.

Christine beams at her. Perhaps that's enough, for now. Worry about the tea later.

"Now look, I'm going to be late – and so are you."

Mrs Markham checks her watch – the strap faded, the delicate glass face knocked in three different places. It's hard to see the hands. One of the few things her ex didn't take on his way out the door five years ago: perhaps he forgot it, or perhaps he knew it wasn't even worth taking to the pawn shop.

"Have a good day then, Mam," says Christine. Her red hair looks messy, unkempt. Has she not brushed it this morning?

"Wait, come here," says Mrs Markham. She smooths her daughter's fringe back, combing it with her fingers and tucking it behind Christine's ears. A black smudge beside her ear also receives a quick rub. There. That's better. Not brilliant, but better. She walks with Christine to the road where, up ahead, the elder two are waiting; Melanie has the day off for a teachers' training day. They'll walk together for no more than two minutes before Wayne and Susan catch the bus to St Hugh's School, their secondary, while Christine will walk for two minutes more to Henderson Avenue Junior.

Mrs Markham waves to the children, turns and begins to rush in the opposite direction. She has no idea why, but at the end of the road she turns. Three figures, two much taller than the third, are just about visible. She hopes they have a good day.

Christine doesn't want to go to school. She has learned, however, to hide this fact – there's power in silence, she's realised. The last thing she wants is to have the other two cotton on: Wayne would tell their mother in an instant. Being nine, though, she has no idea that both Wayne and Susan are well aware she bunks off. It doesn't worry them, because all she's doing is hanging round the newsagents, chatting to shopkeepers and wandering about – checking both ways before she crosses the road. She's no idiot, Christine.

When Wayne and Susan board the bus, Christine waves. "See you later," she calls as the doors close. They watch through the rear window as she turns round smartly and heads back in the direction they came. She might even be going home, using the key their mother hides under the flowerpot. Off she goes down Davy Avenue, swinging her arms, and wondering what she'll do with this day that's hers, all hers.

24

When Mrs Markham returns home to Robinson Close, eight and a half hours later, she finds Wayne and Susan sprawled on the settee. She dashed back in time to ask their neighbour, three doors down, for a little cash – just for the evening. The foreman refused to advance her pay but she'd promised them something nice for tea and was determined to make good. The chips, wrapped in yesterday's newspapers, are heating the inside of her handbag. She couldn't afford a portion each, but it doesn't matter – there's enough. The fish she tucks under one arm as she opens the front door.

"Grab the plates, Wayne," she calls, as she takes off her shoes. Her feet are aching. She can't wait to sit down, to have a cup of tea. Letters lie scattered across the wooden shelf beside the hooks where she hangs the keys. She knows most of these are bills but she hasn't yet been able to open them. She'll do it this weekend. Those brown and white envelopes always look worse than they actually are: their bark – the threat of having the water cut off, or the gas – much worse than their bite.

"Plates!" she shouts into the living room. Why does everything have to be said twice? "Susan, tell your sister to come and eat."

"She's not back yet," says Susan. She's chewing the end of her long plait – a habit from earliest childhood that means she's nervous. Her brown eyes stare at her mother, as though she's waiting for an adult's perspective, a parent's reassurance. But when Christine bunks off – and this Susan knows – she always comes back for her lunch, and she'll usually spend the afternoon loafing around the house.

25

"Not back?" says Mrs Markham. It's almost five o'clock. School finished ages ago. Wayne, reaching for the plates in the kitchen, has frozen.

He's heard the tone in his mother's voice and knows he's for it.

"She wasn't home when you got back from school?"

"No," says Wayne slowly. He looks at his sister. Susan shakes her head very slightly. Nonetheless, he ploughs on. Christine can be so annoying. She never gets into trouble; in fact all she does is succeed in getting him into bother. "But she skived off today anyhow. Didn't go to school."

Susan stares at him, horrified. They're going to be roasted for this.

Mrs Markham stares at her children. They stare back, unsure how this is going to play out. They're ready for an earbashing, a furious interrogation about where their sister goes instead of Henderson Junior, and with whom, and why. But what Margery says, eventually, is far worse.

"I'm going out to have a look. Wayne, call the police."

Christine Markham was small for her age, with red hair, brown eyes and a shy sort of smile. She stood at 3 foot 10 inches. On the day she disappeared, she was described as wearing a red long-sleeved dress, red socks and a blue coat.

That night, 60 volunteers combed the streets around Robinson Close, the school and the surrounding area. The evening of Monday 21st May a torrential flood of rain hit the northeast. The rivers swelled, the streets were pitted with deep puddles; in the parks and commons ponds rose and the ground underfoot became soggy and soft. This prevented the use of police helicopters, which might otherwise have been sent into the skies to search. Specialist underwater teams were directed into the engorged lakes and rivers, peering through the murky depths as the rain pattered persistently on the water's surface.

If Christine had taken shelter that evening, a police spokesman confirmed, she may now have become trapped. By the second day, police confirmed the hideous possibility that had been brewing in the minds of Scunthorpe's residents for close to 48 hours: "If she's trapped she'll have had no food… fears for her health are growing as the search becomes more prolonged. If we're going to find her alive, it will have to be today."

The following day, 22nd May, officers visited Henderson Junior School. They stood patiently before the children, all pale faces and furrowed brows, and asked if anyone had anything to tell them. Had Christine mentioned wanting to run away? Had she been unhappy? Had she mentioned any special friends, any family she might have left to see? Was there anywhere nearby that a friend had visited with her, somewhere that they hadn't yet thought to check?

A timeline was created, revealing what was known or guessed about Christine's movements between the time she'd left home at 8.45am to the various sightings of her before the trail went cold. At 9.10am, she was spotted near the Old Show Ground, Scunthorpe United FC's stadium, which stood on the junction of Henderson Avenue – where Christine's primary school was – and Doncaster Road. It's a Sainsbury's now.

Twenty minutes later, a member of the public reported having given Christine two pounds at the junction of Cliff Gardens and Oswald Road. This was significant. Since the child had asked this member of the public which bus she needed to take to reach Ashby, police speculated Christine may have decided to visit her aunt, Joan Shadlock, who lived on Grange Lane South. Christine had done this before, and always on a Monday. But Joan, her aunt, was on a bus headed in the opposite direction at the time Christine was boarding hers.

At 10am, she was again spotted sitting on a wall near St Hugh's Church in Ashby Road, and at 1pm on Theodore Road, where the Markhams used to live, perpendicular to Robinson Close. The sightings continued right up until 11pm on the day she went missing, when she was seen for the last time at the junction of Davy Avenue and Long Road. Perhaps, ran one theory, Christine had left Scunthorpe to visit a family member who lived with her husband in Norwich. This was checked – she hadn't.

Police dogs roved the streets, the side alleys, the nearby scrubland. This large area of woodland is now a local nature reserve, dotted with oak and birch and scampering rabbits. It's a peaceful sort of place but certainly quiet, remote and seldom accessed on weekdays, apart from dog walkers. Officers from Grimsby and Lincoln were drafted in to help with a coordinated search; 200 members of the force worked together, prodding the ground as they moved slowly through the undergrowth.

On Thursday 24th May, the city's mayor Fred Clarke attended the police's briefing before joining in with the increasingly desperate searches. On Friday, Melanie Markham – Christine's six-year-old sister, was tasked with repeating the walk Christine made on the day of her disappearance.

A red long-sleeved dress and blue coat were selected, and Susan and Wayne walked alongside her as they crossed to the bus stop. Detective Sergeant Jean Dunk walked behind them all, and in a police car, Sergeant Bill Murray advised watching members of the public to please contact them if they'd seen anything at all. "The girl in front with the blue coat is Christine Markham's sister. She looks like the missing girl except that Christine has ginger hair, but she's wearing the same clothes that her sister was wearing when she disappeared last Monday morning. Have you seen Christine?"

Over the next few weeks, 200 phone calls were catalogued from the public, over 2,000 witness statements were recorded and the police were inundated with letters expressing sympathy, concern and sorrow for the Markhams. In the following days, every house within half a mile of Christine's last-seen location was searched, and locals were asked to please check their cellars, attics, outdoor sheds, anywhere that might prove an appealing hiding place for a small child, or one in which she might have come to some sort of accident.

It was also reported that HGVs in the vicinity on the day of Christine's disappearance were located, and their drivers questioned. Perhaps they were afraid to admit they'd agreed to give the girl a lift, or were anxious about confessing they'd allowed a passenger in the cab of their tankers – something that wasn't allowed. Police appealed to them to come forward if they had any information, and not to worry if they had picked her up and dropped her off elsewhere.

By early June, Christine had been missing for two weeks. Police now announced a reward of £200 for information relating to her disappearance. Refuse tips were scoured and excavated in case Christine had fallen or been pushed into a skip and somehow been transported to the local dump. This outcome didn't bear thinking about.

Despite the most intensive investigation ever conducted by the Lincolnshire Constabulary, officers confirmed after a month that there was still no sign of Christine. As the summer holidays approached, locals and visitors alike were reminded of the child through pictures posted at popular sites, and were asked to keep a lookout for anyone matching Christine's description.

The days became weeks and then months, but police were heartened to see volunteers continuing to search. Of course, as time went by, the nature of these searches changed. At some stage, the people of Scunthorpe must have been aware that they were no longer searching for a child who'd fallen, hurt herself, and needed rescuing. Now they were looking for a body.

On 11th June, it was announced that the physical search for Christine was being called off. Unless further information was received, the force simply couldn't go on looking day in, day out – especially without a single scrap of evidence that Christine had come to any harm.

And yet detectives did allude to a line of inquiry focused on the village of Roughton, some 150 miles south east of the industrial powerhouse where Christine lived. One couldn't have imagined two more different places. While Roughton was quiet and rural, Scunthorpe was a hub of activity. But perhaps, as police wondered, there was a connection between the disappearance of their missing girl, walking alone, vanishing without a trace, and the young teen from Norfolk who'd disappeared four years previously.

"I remember that," said a woman in the newsagent's, chatting with a neighbour. "The girl on her bike. Long time ago now. They never did find her, either."

"What was her name again?"

"April."

Christine Markham remains a missing person, presumed dead. DNA has since been collected from her family in case a body fitting her description should ever be found.

Unlike April, Christine was what might then have been called a "troubled" child, a regular truant, and one of many children born to a single mother. She lived not in idyllic Norfolk but in a deprived northern town. The local police force, Mrs Markham's neighbours, her children's friends, rallied to the cause; the media not so much. One might argue that any media fire needs fuel to keep it alive and that the lack of further sightings, evidence or confession effectively killed the story of Christine's disappearance. If this is so, it seems unusual that April Fabb's case – similar in every respect relating to lack of evidence, body or confession – should elicit so much more coverage. So what was stacked against Christine eliciting the same level of response? It would be easier to ask what wasn't.

When children go missing, the first 24 hours are crucial if they're to be found again – especially in abduction cases. In 1973, family photographs were not only helpful: they might prove the difference between a cold case and a solved one. But there were few photographs of Christine, because cameras and the printing of pictures cost money. Only five pictures of the nine-year-old accompanied the missing posters pinned around town. Without these, newspapers would have had no single, captivating image to illustrate the story. There were no bucolic country lanes in Christine's story; her mother had raised her children single-handedly and without much money. April's parents were devout Christians, firmly united, able to stand together at press conferences.

When a child goes missing in a disadvantaged town, what pictures are there to use, besides empty streets and parked cars? And so the public could, should they choose to – consciously or not – see the disappearance of such a child as par for the course. What was she doing, allowed to walk to school on her own? If she'd been accompanied by an adult, she'd still be alive. If her mother had taken her to school, she'd never have been able to vanish.

It wasn't as though Christine went totally unobserved that morning. The sight of a child on a grey weekday morning, especially a young girl alone and with such distinctive red hair, must have seemed unusual. She was seen multiple times, it seems, until that last, late-night spotting. And after that, nothing.

IRELAND, 1977

The jagged border separating the United Kingdom from the Republic of Ireland rises and falls like a wave, like a dorsal fin. In the 1960s and 70s, it was the line over which so much blood was shed, so many families torn apart forever.

The border's power is heighted, perhaps, by its invisibility. There are no wire fences, no guards, no outward evidence of a change from one thing to another. It's an atmosphere, more than anything: a place of change and transformation.

The village of Cashelard lies six miles inland from the North Atlantic coast, a remote and isolated place with fields stretching off into the horizon, a patchwork of vibrancy. It's five miles from Ballyshannon, in County Donegal.

Trees, plants and hedgerows give the impression of paint samples, all different shades of green on a wall pitted with small black circles. These are the loughs, cold and deep, that punctuate the landscape. Further east lies the McNulty Quarry, where vast pits of stone are shifted and sold.

It was here where six-year-old Mary Boyle had spent the day playing with her siblings on her grandparents' dairy farm. The Boyles were on holiday – mother Ann, whose parents owned the farm, father Charlie, eldest boy Paddy and the twins, Ann and Mary. They were excitable, full of energy, happy to be away from home for the St Patrick's Day holiday. It was 18th March 1977.

The land undulates – neither flat nor hilly, it rises and falls in random, skittish fashion, moving from hillocks to wet, sinking swamps. This is land one needs to know well in order to cross it, land that shouldn't be underestimated. Ann and Mary's grandparents could offer the children the most idyllic of playgrounds, provided they were careful. There was 180 acres of space here in which to roam, hide, climb trees and skim stones.

The Boyles had travelled down from their own home in Kincasslagh the day before; an anniversary Mass was being held for an uncle who'd died in a tractor accident some years ago. On the evening before the Mass, the house, not used to accommodating so many, would have bulged if the walls were not crafted from such thick, impenetrable stone.

St Patrick's Day is Ireland's time of celebration, but also of remembrance and memorial. The feast day, 17th March, commemorates the death of the country's patron saint. St Patrick was born in fourth-century Roman Britain but kidnapped at the age of 16 and taken to Ireland – then populated primarily by pagans – to live as a slave. Following his escape, he returned in 432 as a bishop to convert the Irish to Christianity, using – so the story goes – a three-leafed clover as a symbol of the Trinity in his teachings. By the time of his death in 461, he had established many monasteries, churches and schools.

St Patrick's Day in 1977 was a far cry from the atmosphere of revelry and partying that has become synonymous with the feast day in recent years. Before the 1970s, drinking was banned on the public holiday, and since 17th March usually falls within the Christian season of Lent, it was never considered much of an occasion to celebrate – especially not in a pub. For the Boyle family, it was as much a time of reflection and sadness as national pride and spirit: what mattered most was that they were all together.

The Boyles were five of 13 family members who went to bed under the same roof on the night of the 17th. Lizzie and Patrick Gallagher, Mary's grandparents, also hosted their son, Gerry, his wife Eva and their two boys, Gerard and Gregory. It was a sombre occasion made merry by the presence of the kids, eager as always to play with their cousins. The children chased one another from room to room, the sound of slamming doors and dashing feet an accompaniment to the parents' quiet, more thoughtful conversations.

The Gallaghers' farmhouse was the sort of sturdy dwelling intended to survive all manner of weather and keep the elements firmly out. As night fell, the wind whipped through the copse of trees surrounding the house, and branches snapped together like scissors. The noise whistled and moaned through the chimney as the families slept. It had not been a cold day, or indeed month – around eight degrees – but the incessant rain of the past weeks had taken its toll. This was Irish rain; it could soak you to the bone in a matter of minutes. Just a few days earlier, thick fogs had swept in across the desolate landscape, and the only lights to be seen were those twinkling from distant farmhouses just like the Gallaghers'. But here, in the middle of the countryside, they were very much alone. As dawn broke, the lashing wind seemed finally to grow peaceful, the rain cleared momentarily and shafts of sunlight washed over the white stone of the cottage. In the clearing outside the house, all was silent.

On the evening of the 18th, the Ballyshannon Drama Festival was in full swing. That night's performance was *An Trial* by Máiréad Ní Ghráda, a powerful piece of writing set in 1960s Ireland. It tells the story of a single mother's ostracisation following her pregnancy: first by her local community and then in Dublin, as she struggles to support herself and her child. It's not a happy piece of theatre, but a realistic one – educational, insightful and deeply necessary when it was first produced for the stage. Ireland's teenagers still study it as part of the school syllabus.

The evening's gloomy mood was intensified at the play's end, when an usher climbed up onto the stage as the curtain fell. He raised his hands for silence, waiting until the rustle of audience members quietened, until the punters were looking at him curiously. The play was over and they wanted to go home. Whispers punctuated the air but settled as the man raised his voice.

"Thank you for coming tonight, ladies and gentleman," he began. "I hope you enjoyed the performance." He paused. "Now it's a dark night, I know, and a cold one – you'll be wanting to get home. But we've had some news from the Gardaí."

The audience shifted uncomfortably in their seats. News from the Gardaí was an unwelcome if familiar way of life at present. The days were unstable in 1977, a stone's throw from the border. Images flashed before the waiting crowd of streets closed, explosives detonated, some sort of "situation" – euphemistically termed – in motion.

"We've been informed that a little girl's gone missing." The silence deepened. "She's been lost on the mountains since the afternoon. If anyone has a car they don't mind using to help search, or if anyone knows the area well enough, the Gardaí have asked that you join them tonight."

"Whereabouts does she live?" someone in the front row called out.

"It's the Gallagher's granddaughter, Mary. The family were visiting. If any of you know the place, go and head down to help. They're in Cashelard."

Mary Boyle was born in Sparkhill, Birmingham, in 1971. It was the start of a turbulent decade, one characterised by unemployment, strikes and power cuts, the three-day week and Winter of Discontent, rioting, inflation and two disappointing World Cup defeats following the success of 1966. In January alone, 12 IRA bombs were detonated in London.

In the same year as Mary's birth, Britain switched to a decimal currency, abandoning the pounds, shillings and pence of old. The average house cost just shy of £13,000, a pint was 30p and a loaf of bread 20.

By 1972, the Boyles had moved back to Ireland, first to Owey, Charlie Boyle's birthplace, a remote island off the west coast. Charlie worked at a factory, and occasionally as a road worker, while Ann was a bus conductor. Soon enough they'd relocated once more, to Kincasslagh, about a two-hour drive from Ann's parents in Cashelard.

It was a time of huge technological advancement. For the first time, those on even the most modest incomes could save for a colour television, pocket calculator, digital watch or rudimentary computer game.

The year before Mary's disappearance saw the heatwave of 1976, an unprecedented spell of unbelievable warmth, the hottest summer for three centuries. From 23 June until 8 July the British Isles sweltered in temperatures that peaked at 35.9°C. Each day brought fresh reports of the carnage caused by the weather as tarmac melted on motorways and forest fires swept across southern England. Crops failed and food prices skyrocketed.

And then came the ladybirds, all 24 billion of them: an ever-increasing horde of swarming insects. With the intense heat many plants had died, and the ladybirds' main food source, aphids, were dying out too. The food chain was in collapse, so the ladybirds looked for sustenance elsewhere. Some reported the bugs were even attacking humans, settling on sunburnt skin to drink from plentiful supplies of sweat.

Despite the packed lidos and lakes, the sense of ease and sleepiness which pervaded the country, it felt almost apocalyptic at times – not least when the immense heat precipitated a drought lasting until August. At this point the heavens opened and thunderstorms rained down – some of the first rain seen since the winter of 1975, which had been exceptionally dry. Both September and October of 1976 proved extraordinarily rainy and wet. Rivers and reservoirs filled once more.

In Donegal the triangle-shaped lake, Lough Columbkille – a mile round, lying in a mountain hollow – would have received the rainwater emptied into it after the drought and returned to its previous, chilly depths.

The twins Ann and Mary were identical: even close friends found it hard to tell them apart. School photographs show them grinning either side of Paddy, their brother, long dark blonde hair in four neatly plaited pigtails. They were pale, with green eyes and cheeky smiles. What differentiated them was personality, as is so often the case. Ann, the younger, was calm and quiet, shy, somewhat introverted. It was Mary, a feisty child with an adventurous spirit, who did the talking for the pair of them.

On the late afternoon of March 18th, the cousins were playing. As Mary walked out into the garden after tea, she called back to Ann. Was her sister coming too? Ann declined – she wanted to stay behind. She'd help their mother with the dishes, she said.

Mary, dressed in a lilac jumper and brown trousers, pulled on a pair of too-big wellingtons and hopped over the threshold of the door, a flash of white and purple ribbon in her hair. She stood at 3 foot 11 inches, and weighed just under 50 pounds.

The girls' uncle, Gerry Gallagher, was heading out. He needed to return a ladder to the McCauleys, who lived on a neighbouring farm not 800 metres from the Gallaghers' house. He'd borrowed it that morning – a tile was broken on the roof of the farmhouse and, having fixed it, he shouldered the ladder and set off.

Staying behind to help dry plates and spoons wasn't Mary's idea of fun. She skipped after him, across the boggy fields. They squelched through the mud and long grass, feeling their feet pulled down into the many deep swampy indents in the land. The locals called them "swally holes", and they were often covered over with dense piles of leaves.

They walked on for a time, Mary clambering over the stone walls that separated one field from another. The trip to the McCauleys should have taken no more than five minutes each way.

Reaching a particularly muddy patch she paused, looking for a way through. Her uncle was some metres ahead. She called out to him that she was turning back.

*

When Mrs Boyle peered outside in the quickly darkening light, she spotted Paddy – there he was with Gerard and Geoffrey, and there was Ann. Four heads dipped and swooped as they slid over the damp grass, careering into one another.

Four heads when there should have been five. Where was Mary?

The time was a quarter past four. She called to them.

41

"Did Mary come back with your Uncle Gerry?"

No one knew. By the edge of the property, Mrs Boyle spotted her brother, repairing the old stone wall, lifting the heavy blocks one by one. Mary went back, he told his sister later. She didn't want to walk the whole way. Gerry'd remained behind to chat with the McCauleys for no more than half an hour before returning home himself. She should have been back well before him.

The family searched. They called in the dusk, walking further and further around the immediate perimeter of the farmhouse. Charlie Boyle stopped passers-by and neighbours, of whom there were naturally few, to ask them if they'd seen Mary.

At 6pm, they walked out to Lough Columbkille, next to the farm, where a group of fishermen were out on the water for the day. They had a car and agreed to drive the Boyles to Ballyshannon, where they might report Mary missing to the Gardaí. No one had telephones, or any means of contact besides this. If we imagine an hourglass – the golden 60 minutes when information is most likely to be gathered, evidence found or the missing person recovered – that window of opportunity was gradually closing.

The audiences at the Ballyshannon theatre were informed of the search. The town and its surroundings were and remain a tight-knit, protective community and it rallied for the Boyles. The little girl was lost on the mountains. She must have fallen, hurt herself, been unable to walk back for whatever reason. They had to find her.

Bogs and lakes were drained. Six-year-old Ann was tasked with completing a reconstruction of the events leading to Mary's disappearance. But nothing surfaced.

It may seem odd now, but by the following week, a local newspaper reported there was now little chance of finding Mary alive. Perhaps people were accustomed to a more direct, straightforward approach in the 1970s. It's a far cry from the attitude which so heartrendingly dominates today – that of alive until proven otherwise. It would shock any contemporary reader to see reporters voicing such stark attitudes, but they were absolutely correct. The likelihood of any missing person being found alive and well diminishes with each hour they remain unfound.

In Cashelard the terrain was rough, wild and filled with crevices, dark ditches a small child could easily have tumbled down and been unable to climb back up. The lakes were a primary source of interest, of course, but – as the divers' report concluded – "no body recovered".

Unusually, not a single piece of evidence was found. Mary's twin reported that her sister had been eating a bag of crisps when she left with her uncle, but no trace of this was discovered either. No fibre or scrap of brightly coloured clothing, no trace of the ribbon in her hair.

Rumours abounded. Members of the travelling community were suspected of playing some part in her disappearance. Outsiders often come under suspicion before a more likely culprit is suggested.

On Monday 21 March, the *Belfast Telegraph* reported Mary's disappearance. Inspector PJ Daly, who was heading up the investigation, told newspapers over the weekend that there was nothing found, at this stage, to suggest foul play. The story appeared beside that of a young woman from Devon who was struck by lightning on Dartmoor, and another advising farmers in the small town of Cookstown, County Tyrone, to please keep their cattle under control. A number of cows, the article related, had recently been found wandering the local roads.

Ann Boyle, Mary's mother, recalled exactly what she did immediately after realising her daughter was missing.

"I remember in desperation asking my mother to light a candle," she later told journalists. "I shook holy water all over the place."

The Boyles, like most families in the Republic at the time, were deeply religious. Their lives were governed by a devotion to their faith, to attendance at Mass and the teachings of the Pope. Ann Boyle would likely have placed as much hope in God's answering her prayers as in the police.

But the Gardaí, through no fault of their own, were unused to a case like this. Cashelard was a land of swamps and bogs, a desolate sort of place. Most people worked off the land, rearing sheep, growing crops.

The anglers on the lough that day were there illegally: they'd tied fishing lines to nails in a piece of wood and floated it out, waiting for a catch. It was called otter-boarding, and it constituted the severity of crime in the area at the time. It is true that the fishermen would likely have kept a close look-out: eyes swivelling around them, ensuring nobody was coming, and it seemed unlikely they'd have missed cries for help, but who could be sure?

If Mary had been kidnapped, once again it had happened in a matter of minutes. Perhaps her abductor had either planned the crime: biding his time and waiting for the opportune moment, knowing – somehow – that the Boyle family would be staying at the Gallaghers' farm over St Patrick's Day. He would have had to have known that Mary would insist on going with her uncle to return the ladder, a fact impossible to predict. Otherwise, this had been a random attack, a chance decision: he had been extremely reckless, extremely lucky or both.

No evidence of Mary was found between the dairy farm and the McCauleys' property, and as the days turned to weeks, the overriding opinion turned in the direction of a kidnapping. Would the fishermen have taken notice, necessarily, of a car stopping, a door's quick slam?

The other possibility was that Mary had been killed, for reasons unknown, on the stretch of moorland between her uncle's house and the McCauleys'. If this was the case, any perpetrator would have needed much more than the 20 minutes that were available to dispose of the body. There was – quite literally on such a stretch of moorland – nowhere to hide that wasn't searched. The act of digging would have disturbed the earth, something both police and local farmers would have noticed. Fragments of her clothing, or traces of blood, boot-prints in the thick, fresh mud – all would have pointed searchers to what is grimly known as a deposition site. In essence, if Mary was still in or near Cashelard, she would have been discovered.

Over 40 years have passed since Mary's disappearance. There is still no new evidence, no discovery of remains, no body to bury. At St Mary's Church in Kincasslagh, a marble memorial is set into a semi-circular arch of bricks, commemorating the child "who disappeared from her family".

She has been dubbed Ireland's Madeleine McCann, a girl who vanished a decade before the first conviction based on DNA evidence. Police work was still limited, in the late 1970s, by technology that would soon transform the art of detective work. Ditches and bogs were probed with sticks, not thermal-imaging cameras. In recent years, as the internet has democratised access to information, a variety of podcasts, documentaries and online theories have abounded about the case. It seems impossible for a small child to disappear without trace in such a remote area without a single clue as to her whereabouts.

What is certain is that, with the help of family, friends and local people – on top of the Gardaí involvement – the area would have been thoroughly combed. These were folk who knew the swally holes, the many bogs and ditches, the mountainside and its summit. They understood what and where to search, and still they found nothing.

In recent years, fresh reports have pointed to various suspects. With 13 people in residence at Mary's grandparents' house the night before her disappearance, it made sense to start from the inside and work out. Naturally thoughts turned to the Boyles themselves – to Ann and Charlie, the children, to Gerry Gallagher and his wife. Would they – could they – have had a hand in her death?

The same questions surfaced in the wake of Madeleine's disappearance in Portugal in 2007. How, asked the media, could a child simply vanish without a single eyewitness? Why were children of that age left alone, as Madeleine and her siblings were, in an unlocked hotel room? One can imagine the questions raised after Mary's disappearance. When she asked to turn back, would her uncle not have insisted she accompany him, despite the boggy ground? Would he not have walked her home himself?

Mary knew the area; she knew her grandparents' farm. Though a cheeky, outgoing child, she was not, according to family reports, one to wander off. The trip back from the McCauleys' was one she could have done at night, most likely, despite the difficult terrain. It should have taken no more than five minutes. And it is unhelpful to apply the standards of a city-dwelling parent in 2022 to those of a rural community in the late 1970s; times were different. The whole point of the family's move back to Ireland, from the smoky urban jungle of Birmingham, was to ensure precisely the freedom they subsequently allowed their children.

What was almost certainly not on Mary's side was the Troubles, the war being fought a mere hour's drive away. Police forces were stretched to their limits. The year before Mary's disappearance, just 120 kilometres from her grandparents' farm, the Ulster Volunteer Force shot dead six Catholics across County Armagh. In retaliation, the South Armagh Republican Action Force claimed the lives of 11 Protestant men, one of whom – the sole survivor – was shot 18 times.

On St Patrick's Day 1976, four Catholics – including two children – were killed by a car bomb in Dungannon. Not a month went by without further atrocities, and in September the "blanket" protest began; IRA inmates held in the Maze prison in County Down were no longer treated as political prisoners. Their refusal to wear prison uniform encompassed a five-year protest that saw hunger strikes, savage beatings and deaths. The men's refusal to wear uniforms led to the rise of the term "blanketmen": they used the covers from their beds as clothing and, escalating the protest, smeared the contents of their chamber pots on the walls and the floor.

The police were exhausted. 1977 began in appalling fashion, when a 15-month-old baby boy was killed after a car bomb planted by the IRA exploded in Glengormley, near Belfast. A month later, Joseph Morrissey, a 52-year-old Catholic man, was attacked walking home from a club in the centre of Belfast. His was one of the most gruesome deaths reported across the span of the dreadful Troubles: bludgeoned with hammers and knives, he was murdered on the Glencairn Road by the notorious Skanhill Butchers, an Ulster loyalist gang. It was left to his teenaged sons to identify the body, an unrecognisable, disfigured approximation of the man they'd known. When the Butchers were eventually caught, the gang received the longest combined sentences in UK legal history.

Just a week after Mary's disappearance, the IRA planted yet another bomb, in the lecture theatre of north Belfast's Ulster Polytechnic, where Lord MacDermott – the former Lord Chief Justice – was giving a guest lecture. The detonation injured both him and four audience members. Not only were the police focused on these crimes, but the media too. There was a world of difference between 15 civilian casualties in a city centre and one small girl lost on the mountains. No matter how much anyone wanted to help, they were hamstrung by resources, by time and manpower.

The disappearance of Mary Boyle remains Ireland's longest unsolved mystery, a crime that many remember to this day – and for which no one has been brought to justice. The Boyle family are divided, with Ann, Mary's mother, and her remaining daughter now estranged. It has been a long, sad 40 years, made more difficult by the lack of a body to bury, the lack of a single answer to the question of their vanished daughter and sister's whereabouts.

The possibilities fall into three broad categories, as they do for April Fabb and Christine Markham. The first, and the least likely, is that Mary decided to leave on 18th March 1977: she actively elected to run away from home, to leave her family behind. This theory can be discounted almost immediately. How far could she realistically have travelled, on foot, before being found by adults out searching, adults with an intimate knowledge of the area? She could not have arranged to be transported away – she was six. She was also not from Cashelard, but Kinlasslagh, all those miles away. She knew relatively few local people.

49

The second possibility is an accident. Mary's uncle was clearly confident enough about his niece's ability to walk the few minutes back to her grandparents' farm, or he wouldn't have let her go. The ground was uneven and boggy, sodden in places and full of holes down which a small child could fall. But the route between the McCauleys' and the Gallaghers' was scoured. Even before the lakes were fully drained, every possible ditch and bog was probed – the radius extending as the days went by – and the likely path Mary had taken was ruled out. As the divers noted, nothing was found – not even a scrap of clothing, a piece of jewellery, a wellington boot. Science was not, as we know, what it is now. Yet modern-day efforts to locate human remains around the Gallaghers' farm have found nothing.

The third possibility is, of course, the worst. Mary and her uncle set off from the farm together. Gerry Gallagher was the last person to see Mary alive, and he remained at the McCauleys' for a good half hour before returning home – as per his statement to the police. There was a window of time during which Mary was simply unaccounted for. Between turning back on the path to the neighbouring farm and Mrs Boyle realising that Mary had gone, there was time, though for what exactly remains unclear. It emerged that Gallagher was a staunch member of Fianna Fáil, the Republican, conservative political party. Suspicions about him have rent the Boyle family in two, fanned by accusations that he was never formally questioned by the Gardaí – perhaps because, as has been suggested, they'd been instructed to look elsewhere for whoever was behind Mary's disappearance.

For many years, remote County Donegal was known as being precisely the rural, untouched peace Charlie and Ann Boyle had sought out for their children. In recent years, however, reports have emerged of paedophile rings operating primarily in the south of the county – rings that involved and protected various VIPs, businessmen and politicians. What was more, accusers suggest the Gardaí have been complicit in the cover-up. When the possibilities of running away and accidental death have been ruled out, the third option – the most sinister – remains like a terrible, decades-old smell in the air.

In 2005, the year Mary ought to have been celebrating her 44th birthday alongside Ann, tragedy struck the family once more. From June of that year, hurricane season had brought a series of devastating storms – 27 of which were named – to the North Atlantic, the highest number ever recorded until 2020. On 10th July, Hurricane Emily brought with it peak winds of 160mph, strengthening as they moved westwards across the sea. Storms of such power are rare in Ireland, but it does occasionally experience the remainders of a hurricane – the ripple effects –as extra-tropical weather events.

On Monday 18th July, reports emerged that a 12-year-old girl from County Wicklow had drowned, as well as a 22-year-old man in Portrane, County Dublin. It is unknown whether adverse weather conditions contributed to their deaths, but on that day Charlie Boyle, Mary's father, was salmon fishing alone off his native Owey Island. He was an experienced fisherman and had a solid understanding of the water, not least the freezing seas of the North Atlantic during hurricane season. Perhaps being out on the boat calmed him – perhaps it was the one place he felt a measure of peace, after all his family had endured.

By evening he'd failed to return home, and lifeboat services were sent to investigate. He was found, close to his boat in the water, and helicoptered from Burtonpoint Pier. But attempts to resuscitate the 62-year-old at Letterkenny General Hospital failed. He was pronounced dead at 2am the following morning.

CONNECTIONS

There was no reason to connect April, Christine and Mary's cases, besides the fact they were all children, all girls, and all alone when they went missing. April came from a quiet, churchgoing family in rural Norfolk; Christine from a large one in the north of England and Mary from the island of Ireland. The crimes, if indeed any crimes had been committed, were far-flung geographically.

Once the possibility that all had deliberately left their homes had been ruled out, and once the streets, fields, outhouses and sheds had been checked and re-checked, police naturally needed to consider the worst-case scenario. Here, it seems, the children were connected. It was highly unlikely that either April, Christine or Mary actively chose to leave their homes and never come back.

When children are reported missing, the chances of them having been abducted are incredibly low. When this does turn out to be the case, it is far more likely to have occurred as the result of a family dispute. More often than not, parental abduction is the most common cause: a messy divorce and rage-filled arguments over custody arrangements can prompt wild, panicky reactions. According to the charity group Action Against Abduction, in 2016–2017 police in England and Wales recorded more than 200 offences of parental child abduction, and these are just the official figures. For a whole host of reasons, many cases – especially international parental abduction – are not reported to or recorded by police.

And yet once police have ruled out this scenario, other family members, friends, or adults who know the child might come under the spotlight. The majority of all crime – with the obvious exception of drug trafficking and robbery, theft and mugging – is committed by a person known to the victim. The trick, as with everything, is to start close and work your way out.

Abductions by a stranger are rare. There is nothing so horrifying to any parent as the prospect of their child being snatched on the street in broad daylight. It doesn't matter that children are far, far more likely to be hit by cars, have an accident in the playground or contract an illness than suffer a kidnapping, especially one committed by someone unknown. But perhaps because it's the most hideous potential scenario, parents quite understandably fear it much more.

Three quarters of attempted stranger abductions involving children are perpetrated against girls with an average age of 11. For "completed" abduction – with a clear sexual motive – the average age of victims rises to 14, and two thirds are committed using a vehicle of some kind.

Such cases represent the very worst-case situation for investigators. Without witnesses, without number plates, without the

CCTV cameras we have come to associate with the modern jigsaw assembly of a criminal case, it is very challenging to track an abductor. The "golden hour" immediately following such a crime is aptly named. It's the time frame in which a child is most likely to be recovered following a kidnapping, the time in which most evidence can be gathered – fast, while memories are still fresh – and acted upon.

It stands to reason that any abductor, especially one who has committed a crime on the spur of the moment, would attempt to flee the scene of the crime as fast as possible. They will be keen to place distance between themselves and whatever has happened, between themselves and potential eyewitnesses. They rely on that golden hour as much as the police do, but for wildly different reasons. For both April and Christine, that crucial hour was missed. By the time their disappearances were reported to police, any potential abductor had the time to travel tens if not hundreds of miles.

What is most frightening about stranger attacks is that the majority of kidnappings are planned. The abductor will have watched their intended victim for some time, formulated a plan and executed it. They may well have been lurking, unnoticed, for several months before the crime takes place. It's not uncommon for this perpetrator to have committed similar, if smaller-scale, offences in the past. As with most crime, it's unusual for an abductor to begin with a large-scale attack. Most likely it has been brewing for some time, perhaps manifesting in stalking behaviour, attacks on animals, arson, domestic abuse and other forms of violence.

But rarest of all is the random attack: the abduction that takes place without planning, without forethought, a true crime of opportunity. For police, this represents the needle in the haystack, the most urgent but also the most indecipherable. Where do they begin?

What is certain is that crimes such as these, however seldom they occur, have tragic consequences for small and larger communities alike. Whether it's a village like April's or a larger town like Christine's, all anybody wants is a resolution – however awful that resolution might be.

Police begin by questioning those closest to the missing child – her parents, siblings, friends, grandparents, teachers. It is perhaps understandable that the families of missing children so often experience the worst kind of isolation as a result, with some members of the community pointing the finger and others falling under suspicion themselves. Suspects may be brought in for questioning, interrogated and released – their clean records and cast-iron alibi having little effect on a frantic street's desire to cast them as the villain.

Some facts might be established, though, especially in April and Mary's cases. These were remote, rural areas where strangers were often noticed. But perhaps they might not be so visible during holiday seasons – like Easter, or St Patrick's Day. If local suspects are eliminated, then investigators must consider the possibility of a day-tripper, a tourist: somebody who, whether by chance or on purpose, entered a community and left it just as quickly. Since the bodies of these children were never recovered, it also stands to reason that they were buried or otherwise disposed of elsewhere, perhaps many hundreds of miles from where they were taken. An abductor acting on impulse may well panic, deciding to cover his tracks by getting as physically far from the scene of the crime as possible.

This is extraordinarily rare. In the most tragic, desperate incidents of abduction and murder – those involving either children or adults – bodies are more often discovered close to wherever the attack took place.

Dr Angela Gallop CBE is one of the country's leading forensic scientists. She has written extensively about the need for investigators to examine a crime scene with the utmost care and attention; she cut her teeth on the infamous Yorkshire Ripper cases, a complex and ever-changing training ground.

"Getting as clear a picture as possible of the likely sequence of events," she writes, "tells you what the forensic opportunities might be and enables you to plan the most effective strategy for testing.[1]" She came to realise how almost all the clues necessary for effective testing remained, waiting, at the scene of a crime. It's vital that scene investigators are properly trained, however, to search for those clues.

It was almost impossible, back in the 1960s and 1970s, for police to comb for evidence with the sort of knowledge modern-day officers would make use of – in Christine Markham's case, there was no clear crime scene anyway. But in the cases of April Fabb and Mary Boyle, there were final sightings, an abandoned bicycle, a very limited area in which a crime might have taken place. But police can only search for evidence if they know what they're looking for.

Locard's principle, formulated by the so-called "French Sherlock Holmes" Dr Edmond Locard, is the idea that every contact leaves a trace. Whenever a perpetrator arrives at a crime scene, they will both bring something to it and take something away from it, in forensic-science terms.

"Wherever he steps, whatever he touches, whatever he leaves, even unconsciously, will serve as a silent witness against him," said the microscopy specialist Paul L Kirk. "Not only his fingerprints or his footprints, but his hair, the fibres from his clothes, the glass he breaks, the tool mark he leaves, the paint he scratches, the blood or semen he deposits or collects. All of these and more, bear mute witness against him. This is evidence that does not forget. It is not confused by the excitement of the moment. It is not absent because human witnesses are. It is factual evidence. Physical evidence cannot be wrong, it cannot perjure itself, it cannot be wholly absent. Only human failure to find it, study and understand it, can diminish its value.[2]"

It is likely that in the cases of April Fabb and Mary Boyle, trace, fragmentary evidence did indeed exist. If the science had been advanced enough, April's bicycle could well have provided enough information for police to apprehend the person responsible before he or she acted again. In Mary's case, the boggy, wet soil of Donegal would likely have retained shoe-impressions, unless the perpetrator took the immense risk of delaying his getaway by concealing them.

It's one thing to know and understand Locard's principle, of course, but quite another to apply it. In the past, investigators have been faced with the challenge of evidence that is too microscopic to test, let alone find in the first place.

Nowadays, a suspected scene – however big or small – is cordoned off until police photographers have been able to document exactly what the area looks like, sometimes using video cameras. The wood or wire of fences is combed meticulously for traces of clothing, caught wisps of human hair, a single drop of blood, a scrape of paint.

The manner of the girls' disappearances was stacked against them from the start: few if any witnesses, a delay between their abductions and wide-scale searches – but it was also hampered by the lack of ability to find what police needed. Surely it was there: they just couldn't see it.

Just two years before Mary's disappearance, on Christmas Day 1975, UK audiences flocked to see a film that soared straight to number one at the box office. Cinema staff watched amazed as queues snaked their way round street corners for this eagerly anticipated story. The film had quickly become famous in America – the most successful in movie history, in fact – and audiences had spent the summer in a state of hysteria the likes of which had never been seen before.

Peter Benchley's novel *Jaws* had been published the year before to great success, and remained on the bestseller lists for almost a year. Film producers quickly snapped up the novel's rights and selected Steven Spielberg to direct the adaptation. The blockbuster was shot and released in record time; cinemas sold programmes and soundtrack tapes in the foyers, and a generation of kids were scared out of ever dipping so much as a toe in the sea.

The film was not slated to do as well as it did. It was a creature-feature, after all – hardly a mainstream affair – and a horror film to boot. It wasn't seen as "highbrow", cultural, ground-breaking. At its heart, the elevator pitch was deceptively simple: it's the tale of a killer shark, slinking its way silently along the heavily populated beaches of an American summer resort. People who believed themselves to be safe were shocked to discover the opposite, and authorities failed to recognise the similarities between a series of brutal attacks. It all seemed so odd, so out of the ordinary.

Brody, the town's police chief – notoriously terrified of swimming – takes matters into his own hands. Enlisting the help of an experienced local fisherman and a marine biologist, he sets out to capture and kill the shark once and for all, thereby putting an end to its reign of terror and saving the summer season for locals and tourists alike.

As the film critic Mark Kermode has written, *Jaws* is not a film about a shark – not really. "It may have a shark in it," he comments, "and indeed all over the poster, the soundtrack album, the paperback jacket and so on[3]" – but it isn't about a shark. It's about a small town terrorised by something unseen, something hidden. The most sinister, eerie moments of the film come not from the shark, but from the citizens of Amity, and from the three men who set out to try and capture the beast. Indeed, as one character relates from a night spent waiting for rescue in a shark-infested sea, the real fear comes from the unknown. Who would be next? Would they survive? How dreadful to know that a threat is present, but to feel so utterly helpless to prevent its occurrence.

The terror in all good horror films stems from very simple questions. What is this, and where has it come from? What does it want? Once some of these are answered, the sinister loses its sting. Cinema audiences of the 1970s may have recoiled from the black, soulless eyes of the shark as it reared its head at Chief Brody, but the fear was so much worse before they knew what it was.

Part Two

"May She Someday Be Returned"

EXETER, 1978

The M5 runs in a curving line from the Midlands to the South West. It begins near Birmingham, in the country's centre, and snakes down towards Exeter, in Devon. The motorway was built in sections, the first being a 26-mile stretch ending just north of Cheltenham. This was completed in 1962 and marked a turning point in the history of British transport. Those with cars were now able to travel on a road specifically designed for speed; the future had arrived, and it was about to transform the way that people in England commuted and lived.

Over the next 15 years, work continued on the M5, this new road threading its southward journey through Gloucestershire and Somerset all the way to Exeter. This novelty represented the first easy-access gateway to the South West the country had seen. The motorway system across the UK was a relatively new phenomenon. The first was opened in 1958 – the Preston Bypass, now part of the M6 –followed by the M1 in 1959.

These smart, long, open sweeps of fresh tarmac became tourist destinations in themselves, and there were no speed limits. In the 1960s, their construction intensified, leading to the Ministry of Transportation classifying A and B roads to join the M class. By 1970, 1,000 miles of motorway had been built. These new highways were not without notoriety, however, with many environmentalists protesting at the destruction of forestry, farmland and agricultural space which the new roads necessitated.

The tiny village of Aylesbeare stood just five miles east of the M5, this busy new road, the interlinking thoroughfare with the rest of the country. It must have been a relief to some of its residents, having the road nearby – but not too close. They wouldn't be able to hear the roar of motor vehicles all that way away, but they could zip onto the motorway's fast lanes into Exeter or beyond should they need to.

Aylesbeare was and remains a farming parish. Approaching from the southern road, along Village Way, pretty houses stand either side of a well-kept lane. At the top of this winding street one can see the village's oldest building: dedicated to the Blessed Virgin Mary, the church dates back to the 13th century. On the right-hand side of a dead-end track it seems tucked away, nestled cosily beside solid-looking houses. A kissing gate opens onto the churchyard; the slanted roofs lead to a tower, its little turrets and circular lookout-post giving it a fairy-tale air.

On entering the church, the font on the left-hand side provides a sort of display area for local crafts, and is often decorated during festivals for children. Stained-glass windows pay tribute to the village's former bakeries, cobbler's, black-smith and cider-makers.

In 1975, the motorway was complete. Previously hard-to-reach hamlets and villages were now much more accessible, and day-trippers might jump in the car for a pleasant weekend tour of the pretty surroundings.

At this point in time there were four new residents of Barton Farm Cottage, a smallholding close to the centre of the village. John Tate and his wife Violet were newly-weds, each with a daughter from their previous marriages. Both children lived primarily with the couple. Violet's daughter Tania was around the same age as John's daughter Ginny. The newly formed family unit was adjusting to life together.

It was a somewhat modern arrangement, and one that appears to have worked quite well, given the circumstances. Blended families like the Tates were uncommon; Tania maintained regular contact with her birth father, and Ginny with her mother, who now lived in Bristol. The arrangement seemed a happy, harmonious one – but in 1970s Devon, it would have been unusual to see this disparate group getting along so well, making it work.

Born in Somerset on 5th May 1965, Ginny had lived with her parents in a suburban district of the county called Wedlands, before relocating briefly to Cornwall. When John and his first wife separated, he and Ginny moved to Devon, where he worked as a sales representative. Part of the reason for this separation of mother and daughter – again, an unusual choice at the time – was John's health.

He'd suffered from a rare form of muscular dystrophy since birth and, although the disease "hardly affected" him, it was a hereditary illness. Ginny was found not to have inherited it, but John and Sheila decided not to risk having another child in case they both carried and suffered from the condition. "I couldn't in my heart help to bring into the world someone who would be unable to play sport, to run, walk or participate in an ordinary everyday life," wrote John in his memoirs. "When my first marriage broke down it was because of all this that Genette was left in my care, Sheila not having the heart to part us. From that moment on Genette became ever more important."[4] It's possible John and Ginny used the new road on their approach to Aylesbeare when they arrived in 1975. Certainly they would have joined it on the way to visit Sheila, Ginny's birth mother, an hour's drive away. Barton Farm Cottage was one of several farmhouses a stone's throw from the village centre. It was cosy-looking, with a green and vibrant garden filled with flowers.

Aylesbeare is a non-descript, peaceful sort of place: the majority of its 500 residents in the mid-70s worked on farms, as they had done for generations, or in neighbouring villages; the city of Exeter also provided opportunities for employment. Many retirees came to the village for a quiet life, but there were increasing numbers of commuters to Exeter Airport cropping up in the lanes and side roads. To this day, it's possible to drive in and out of the village in under a minute, passing the church, the pub, the phone box.

At the Tate household, life was happily unremarkable. The village may have seen a little more traffic than before, but geography was on its side. It was impossible for two cars to pass one another at the same time on the lanes, which slowed their speed to a crawl. Even on a bicycle, one or the other would need to give way. It was never a rat-race – there would be few reasons to travel through Aylesbeare, and residents could allow their children to play outdoors for miles around without fear of accident.

John Tate was a softly spoken man, with a classic 1970s mop of hair accompanied by a full beard, thick-rimmed glasses and sharp, shrewd eyes. Born at the height of the Second World War, his was a childhood of rationing, making do and mend, of news bulletins over the wireless. He would have watched the soldiers returning from battle, weary and scarred. Any parent would have been grateful for the relative stability of his own child's life – the lack of omnipresent fear, of disruption and scarcity. And John's daughter Ginny had such a life. She and Tania were as free as children could be in the 1970s, in a small Devon village. Life, the family said, was harmonious.

The photograph of Ginny used by the media will be well-known to many across the UK. For reasons unknown, press coverage used two school pictures taken a full four years earlier. These images show a beaming child smiling cheekily at the camera, her collar starched and prim, her hair cropped short like a boy's, her front teeth visible, still growing. This was the girl splashed across the front pages, the one everybody searched for. This was Genette Tate.

"Genette is 5 foot tall, with short brown hair and brown eyes, suntanned, and looks her age", read the description issued on Monday 21st August 1978.

Ginny was 13 when she went missing. In the last photograph taken with John she is seated at a bus stop, panes of glass keeping the rain off local notices pinned to a corkboard.

John is smiling, wearing a dark brown shirt, jeans and slim, shiny brogues. He is grinning at Ginny. She's looking directly at the camera in a pink, spotted bandanna, black cardigan and high-waisted beige trousers. Like her father's beside her, the bottoms of her trousers are flared. She looks cool, more like a contemporary East London student than a country girl in the 1970s. John and Ginny's legs are touching, and they have an almost identical posture: hands planted on knees, sitting upright. Their sleeves are rolled up to their elbows. Who knows where they were going, or who took the photo. The public didn't see this image of Ginny until much later. For some time, it was assumed she was much younger – certainly under 10.

She was a bright and curious child, not especially outgoing or demonstrative, but kind and interested. "I well remember her scrutinising a worm in the garden when she was one,"[5] wrote John some years later. She enjoyed learning and was inquisitive, especially when it came to animals. She wrote poetry and liked being with her friends from school – though often quiet, she was a careful observer, sweet-natured and loyal. She sang in the village choir, took her dog for a walk each day and was a member of the Girl Guides.

At 13, she was likely in the no-man's land of her early teenage years: she had recently started dating a local boy, Tony, and might well have experienced her first sip of beer, a breathless puff of a filched cigarette, or bought her first record. These were the last days of real childhood, though, when she might still play with old toys, pick up a much-loved picture book or slyly pinch a sugar cube from a bowl on the table.

In recent years her parents had noticed a particular aptitude for Maths. There seemed some knowing, under-stated intuition to the way she handled numbers, balanced equations and simplified fractions. Her abilities had "amazed the family from a young age".[6]1978 saw the coolest August for 12 years, all rain and showers. Towards the end of the month, higher pressure prevailed and the sun did occasional-ly manage to peek through. The country was gripped by the recently released *Grease!* film, and "You're The One That I Want" was in the top five.

On Saturday 19th August the Tate household was up and about by 6.30am – Violet, Ginny's stepmother, was working and John had agreed to drive her in. Not a long journey by any stretch – they left at 7.30am and, after dropping off his wife, John bought petrol and attended a doctor's appointment in nearby Woodbury at 9.20am. By 10am both Tania and Ginny had emerged from their bedrooms, sleepy-eyed and hungry. When John returned he made breakfast for them both, and once they'd eaten and dressed, the pair set off for the post office, where they bought sweets.

Increasingly, this untouched corner of south-west England was becoming a tourist mecca. The locals were less than pleased – referring to the incomers as "grockles" and "emmets". The quiet lanes and calm tranquillity of endless woods and fields was proving more and more of a draw for city-dwellers keen for a country break in rural England.

Like many young teenagers keen to earn a little extra cash, Ginny had a paper round. On 19th August she would be delivering in Perkin's Village, just a mile and a half from Aylesbeare. She was covering that week for a local boy who was on holiday and couldn't make his usual round; this Saturday was to be the last day. The job wasn't taxing and Ginny had chosen to take it independently of her parents. A little extra pocket money and a few afternoons out on her bike at the height of summer seemed a fair trade for delivering some newspapers.

That evening, Violet's daughter Tania and her boyfriend were planning to stay with Tania's birth father. It wasn't a long journey, but they would be travelling by coach to stay for a fortnight in Cornwall. John was once again serving as chauffeur and would drop them in Exeter to catch the coach.

Ginny remained behind, immersed in her puzzle books. Her father set off with Tania, waving to his daughter as she lay on the lawn, frowning over a page of riddles and crosswords, her head down. She was wearing light-brown trousers – possibly the same ones seen in the photograph with John – white plimsolls and a white cotton T-shirt. The top was embroidered in red stitching across the left shoulder, spelling out her name.

John later recalled waving goodbye to his daughter as she reclined with her books. She waved back, and then he was gone.

At around 2.30pm, Ginny wheeled her bicycle out onto the lane and began her round. She cycled south west to a bus stop within sight of the White Horse Inn, collected around 70 newspapers from a van and started her route. She delivered the first set of papers to the village of Farringdon, collecting payment as she went. With each posting of a paper the bicycle basket became lighter, the steering easier.

By half past three, she had already delivered around 14 newspapers, and was wheeling her bike along Withen Lane. The road leading from Perkin's Village back up to Aylesbeare is steep and long, hard work for a child and especially one as laden as Ginny was. Nonetheless she made good progress.

The still country air was pierced by the sounds of greeting – at this point, precisely 3.28pm, Ginny ran into Margaret Heavey and Tracey Pratt, who went to her school and lived in the village. By now they were at the most remote part of the lane, standing on a small bridge over a stream. On the other side of the tiny road, a mother and her daughter were throwing sticks into the water and smiled at them all good-naturedly.

The girls were friends and ran into one another often, even when they'd not arranged to meet.

"How many more do you have?" Margaret asked, pointing at the basket.

"I'm nearly finished," Ginny said. "About another 20, I reckon."

"Can we take one?" Tracey asked, and Ginny nodded. It wasn't a hot day, but the ride to Perkin's and the steep climb had tired her. She wanted to go home and rest again, eat some sweets, draw or write. Soon she'd be finished.

Tracey turned the page and suddenly her eyes lit up. "Look," she gestured to the second page. "Another UFO!"

Ginny laughed. It was true – the newspaper featured a story that week about a possible alien sighting nearby. The *Express and Echo* was, at the time, a daily broadsheet-style paper; established in 1904, it was a merger between the *Western Echo* and *Devon Evening Express*.

It was filled with local stories, notices and advertisements. In a pre-internet age, when not everyone had access to televisions or even radios, people relied on such dailies for their updates.

The story that so fascinated the two other girls ran with a headline reading *UFO-tograph… an encounter of the Flying Dutchman Kind.* The picture was captioned with an explanation that a transport plane had been landing at Exeter Airport at the same time as the supposed alien spacecraft was spotted – and although the lights were most likely from the plane's landing gear, the possibility that photographic evidence of life beyond Earth had been proved had stoked the reporter into a frenzy. The light's "pulsating" brightness was referenced as evidence of something otherworldly. It's possible that Ginny herself, waiting for one client or another to pop back inside for their purse, might have perused the story herself. Perhaps she believed it; perhaps she chuckled.

Ginny continued past, pushing the heavy bike while the girls, spellbound, waved her on and settled down on the verge to read. As the road bent, she climbed back onto her bicycle, called goodbye to her friends and pedalled off.

Seven minutes passed. Birds cawed in their branches, and the lush green leaves of tall trees bent in a slight breeze. In the distance, a motor, an engine, then silence again. Tracey and Margaret were in deep discussion on the topic of UFOs. Since the late 1960s, when Neil Armstrong and his fellow astronauts made global history walking on the moon, space had become universally fascinating, and this pair of teenagers on a quiet country lane in Devon were no different.

The girls rounded the bend, heading towards the top of Withen Lane and back to the centre of the village.

"Here what's that?" asked Tracey, pointing up ahead. The sun was reflecting off something metallic, a glint they couldn't quite make out.

"It's moving," said Margaret. "Looks like a wheel – I think it's spinning?"

"It's a bike," said Tracey. "Ginny must've come off. Quick."

Together they raced up the hill, past the bracken and overhanging branches, the chirruping of crickets. The bike lay on its side, the papers strewn across the warm tarmac of the road.

The girls stood for a moment, looking down, before turning around.

"Where is she?"

"Ginny?"

John had dropped his stepdaughter at the coach station in Exeter before heading back to the hospital to collect his wife.

They'd done a little shopping and taken a walk around the city centre, stopping outside the cathedral for an ice cream. Staff at Dingle's, a local department store, recalled John collecting a plate bought to replace one that had been broken at home.

Around half an hour after the discovery of the bicycle, John and Violet returned to Barton Farm Cottage. Outside, they found Ginny's two friends waiting outside. Strangely, they were sat by the front door.

"She's not here, Maggie," John said. "She's out on her paper round this afternoon."

"Mr Tate, we saw her – we saw Ginny." Margaret's face was flushed, her eyes anxious. "She went off on her bike and then we came along at the top of the lane and we found it."

Now John's eyes flicked to the left and saw it, the blue of the saddle bright in the late-afternoon light: Ginny's bike, leaning against the house. "I rode it home," said Margaret in a small voice.

By 5pm, John and Violet – having begun the search with friends and neighbours – conceded they needed extra help. The light was still strong and would be for several hours yet. There was often a simple explanation when it came to teenagers, John told himself. What bothered him was the bike, its position, the papers strewn across the lane. Ginny would never just leave her bike like that. And if she'd been struck by a car, left with a head injury, she might be concussed, confused, wending her way through lanes and villages as she struggled to understand where she was. Slowly, darkness began to fall, recalled John Tate:

"...and with it the rain. I imagined Genette staggering in a daze – the rain having woken her up somewhere. So I drove around and around, country lane after country lane. Once, when I got back to the village, I met a group of people who were searching in the darkness with only two torches. Oh God, let the rain stop."[7]Before it was decided that detectives themselves needed training in the field of crime-scene preservation, Scenes of Crime Officers (SOCOs) were civilians. They'd approach with the most basic arsenal at their disposal and, although things were soon to change, county forces generally were unprepared for the complexity and apparent lack of evidence such as that on Withen Lane in 1978. There was little in the way of preservation and a SOCO might never have been tasked with packaging, for instance, a pedal bicycle: most likely a tarpaulin was procured to cover it, but issues of cross-contamination were rarely considered, and by this point the girls Maggie and Tracey, who had touched the bike, would also need to be eliminated from inquiries. Whatever evidence remained was trace: too small for the human eye to see, mere microns. In the late 1970s SOCOs didn't even wear paper suits to prevent further contamination.

Time had been lost, but not too much. By 6pm the police were out in force, combing the hedges and trekking across the fields, searching for any sign of the missing 13-year-old. Tracker dogs were given items of her clothing and set off, bounding along Withen Lane, pausing where the bike had fallen and then scouring the ground nearby, their noses pressed to the ground. A major incident was declared. John

Tate's movements were checked and re-checked. "I had to have an alibi just the same as anybody else," he remarked at the time, "and they were satisfied with where I'd been and what I said I'd done."

Canine tracking was in use across British police forces by the late 19th century. Then, as now, it's all in the nose: a dog's has 300 million olfactory receptors, 294 million more than a human. What's more, the portion of a dog's brain responsible for smell is almost 40 times as large as a human's. They are therefore extremely useful in identifying "matches", able to distinguish between – for instance – tiny particles of scent left behind by Margaret and Tracey, who were in the same vicinity at the same time, and Ginny's own scent. These incredible dogs are able to reject extraneous smells, focusing in on the specific scent being sought. In addition, they are able to track how this scent moved, where it went and when it stopped. Possibly the most famous was Rex, a stray rescued from a police base and trained as a search-and-rescue dog during the Second World War. Volunteers from the Women's Auxiliaries gradually worked the trainees up to dealing with everything from fireworks, bangers and thunder-flashes, ensuring they wouldn't run from gunfire.

Rex was one of 30 dogs sent to the Royal Engineers: the last platoon of mine-sweeping dogs formed during the conflict. He even travelled to France following D-Day, and on March 3rd 1945, he saved many lives by finding more mines than any other dog. In April of that year, he received the People's Dispensary for Sick Animals' Dickin Medal, established to honour the work of animals during the war. Rex, it was noted, had displayed "outstanding good work", not only in the minefields of Germany's deep forests, but also finding injured soldiers and civilians in burning buildings. Following human scents, he would bring people to safety.

In Devon, the dogs worked late into the evening but discovered little. The scent left behind by Ginny did not extend further than where her bike was discovered, suggesting it was unlikely she had left it deliberately and had walked further either up or down Withen Lane.

Officers from neighbouring districts were called in to help with the search, plus an RAF helicopter. Mounted police from Avon and Somerset also trotted through the lanes, circling further and further from the site of Ginny's last-known location.

John Tate sat in his living room. Violet was in the kitchen making them both a cup of tea. It was 11pm.

"Here you are, love," she said, putting it gently beside him on the coffee table.

He stared into the distance, seeming not to notice his wife.

"John," she said. "Look at me."

He glanced up, blinked and managed a tired smile. "Sorry. I'm here."

"Drink your tea."

Violet rubbed her eyes. It seemed incredible that leaving for work, doing her shift, meeting John afterwards, the sweet hit of strawberry ice cream in the square – that this had all happened today. It felt like weeks ago, months even.

The atmosphere in the house had shifted, changed its shape. Everything looked different now, like milk left out too long in the sun – hot and close and curdled.

Tania was to stay at her father's for the time being. They'd managed, briefly, to speak in between the searches.

"You're best out of the way, away from all this," Violet had told her daughter. "It's chaos, Tan."

Tania was crying down the phone; Violet could hear the short, sharp intakes of breath.

"She wasn't even wearing a helmet, Mum," she said. "She never took it with her. What if she's just lying there in a ditch somewhere with her head split open? I can't –"

"Tania," Violet said sternly. "She's not in a ditch. We've looked, of course we've looked. And if she came off her bike she'd be nearby. Can't you see that? We checked everywhere all around. Even if she'd been thrown a hundred metres into the air, one way or the other, we'd have found her."

This was, Violet realised immediately, the wrong thing to say. Tania cried harder than ever. "But if she wasn't knocked off the bike, where is she? What the hell's happened to her? I want to come home, Mum."

"You can't," Violet said. She steeled herself for a fight, but Tania, it seemed, didn't have much more of one to give. "There's too much going on here right now. The police are in and out, they've been in her bedroom, collecting some of her things. And we're setting off again in a moment to check the route one more time before the morning. It's easier for me to have you there, with your dad."

"Ok," Tania replied, in a small voice.

"Now listen Tania," Violet said kindly, "Will you put him on for me?"

Tania muttered a goodbye and then the phone was placed down briefly before being picked up again.

"Violet? What's the news? Any sign of her yet?"

Violet smiled sadly at the sound of her ex-husband's voice. He was a sweet man, good-natured, kindly. They'd fought like dogs towards the end, but she loved him – more so perhaps since they'd separated. He'd never shown the slightest jealousy when she remarried, and in fact Violet suspected that, were circumstances different, he and John might actually get on quite well. And he was a good dad to Tania – the sort who'd feel, even more than Tania herself, the immense pain she and John were enduring.

"Still nothing," Violet said into the receiver, more quietly now. "We're leaving in a moment to start again. How's Tania?"

"Well, you heard her. She's upset. Says she's heard about little girls vanishing off the streets and she knows what happens to them."

Violet frowned, her eyes closing briefly, willing the images away.

"But I also told her that Aylesbeare's hardly that sort of place, now, is it? Something's happened to the poor thing, no doubt about it, but I'm sure she'll be along home tonight. She have a boyfriend?"

"Yes, a local lad," said Violet. Tony was a sweet boy. He and Ginny had only been dating a few months.

"Well, have they spoken to him?"

"Of course – but he's only 13, and he wasn't even out this afternoon anyway."

"They might have made plans to run off together, and then he's bottled it and she's gone ahead ready to meet him somewhere?"

"Yes, we thought of that, but he swears not." Violet looked over her shoulder at the silent figure of John in his armchair. "But it's the bike, you see. All those newspapers across the ground." She said this quietly, wishing she'd closed the living room door.

"That makes no sense," he agreed. "Well, look. Keep us updated. Don't worry about Tania: I'll look after her. Just focus on finding Ginny."

"Thank you. I'll phone again tomorrow."

"And Violet?" she heard his voice coming loud and clear from the receiver, just as she was about to replace it in the cradle. "Take care of John. Lord knows he must be in hell right now."

Hell was one word for it, thought Violet, as she crossed back into the living room. But then hell suggested some element of pain, of recognition, devastation. Here before her was a man devoid of all emotion, a man shocked into a still and disturbing silence.

"John?" she touched his shoulder briefly. He smiled up at her now, his eyes glassy as a doll's.

"What did Tania say?" he asked mechanically. His hair was wild, stuck up at all angles, and his trousers were streaked with mud and grass stains.

"She's upset. She'll stay with her dad, though. He sends his best to you."

"That's good of him," said John. "Tell him thanks when you next speak."

He sounded so robotic, still, so exhausted.

"Do you think it'd be an idea to sleep for an hour or two?" she asked. "Not much we can do at night, and we'll need our strength for tomorrow."

"For tomorrow," repeated John. It sounded as though he couldn't believe it, as though it was impossible tomorrow would come at all.

There came a knock at the door, soft and tentative. John didn't appear to hear it. Violet stood and walked through the hallway, past Tania's glittery summer sandals, Genette's sports shoes from school, John's heavy black boots, her own wellingtons. She stared at them for a second, then bent to straighten the wellies. Mud had crusted their bottoms; she'd need to smack them together outside before they set off.

She turned back to the door, opened it and stared out into the dark yard. Their little enclosure was like a farmer's paddock, the houses close knit and accessible by one main gate onto the road. She couldn't see anyone.

On the step before her, a tin cooled under embroidered muslin, a cake in a little wire basket beside it. There was no note. She stared at the items before picking them up, one by one, and bringing them into the kitchen. On the table sat a cereal bowl, dregs of milk and oats floating on the edges, a plastic tumbler of water beside it. She was always telling Ginny to wash up her dishes once she'd used them.

"Actually, let's go," she called back to the living room. The house seemed suddenly hot, overwhelming, close. She couldn't breathe. "John? Let's go."

She heard him stand, heard his strange, jerky walk over to the front door. She watched him pull on a thick black coat, sit on the bottom step of the stairs to lace his boots and finally extract a heavy torch from the understairs cupboard. He switched it on once, sharply, and its beam filled the hallway. "Ok," he said, "I'm ready."

They walked across the yard together, not speaking, their feet crunching across the gravel. A policeman stood in the lane outside, his hands behind his back. He nodded to them shyly as they passed. No more than a boy himself, really. He didn't seem to know what to say to them.

They turned onto the street, usually so quiet at this time of night. It was almost midnight now but the air was bright with torchlight, with windows blazing, and all around them came noise and conversation, shouts and orders. The pub was open late, though no one could be seen inside its thick, ancient windows.

As they crossed through into the next field over, John and Violet were met with the sight of villagers, all of them shining their torches, crossing over the field in formation, shouting Ginny's name. John turned abruptly and Violet followed. "Not now," he muttered. "I can't speak to them now."

And so they walked to Withen Lane, to the spot where the bicycle was found. Here again they found a policeman, an older one this time, standing guard over the spot where the *Express and Echos* had been scattered.

"Have they found anything?" asked Violet. It was becoming chilly. She thought of Ginny, out here alone somewhere, and realised as she asked the question that she didn't much want to know the answer.

"Nothing as yet, Mrs Tate," said the officer. "We've had the helicopters out, though. If she's here, we will find her." The policeman's eyes wandered over to John, standing stock still beside the hedgerow. "You can leave it with us, Mr Tate. We're doing everything we can."

"Oh, I know, I know," said John. "Don't mind us." He seemed to chuckle ruefully then, sounding almost like himself, Violet thought. "We just didn't feel right sitting indoors all night."

"I understand," said the officer. "Look, there's a team of volunteers heading to Perkin's in a moment. Maybe you could join them? We know she delivered some of the papers there, so perhaps a clue —"

"I want to stay here, if that's alright," said John. And with that, he sat down at the side of the lane, staring straight ahead. For 20 minutes there was silence until, somewhere in the distance, in the canopied ceiling of trees over the little bridge, an owl began to hoot.

"John, come on," said Violet. "We have to keep moving. Stand up."

"She's not here," said John. The police officer's head turned sharply.

"What do you mean?" He was suddenly alert, agitated, eyeing the other man with a sudden and frightening intensity. "Do you know where she is?"

"Of course he bloody doesn't," said Violet, alarmed by the officer's change in stance and tone. His hand had moved imperceptibly to his belt. "He has no idea where she is."

"You're half right, Vi," John said. He stared around him at the hedges on either side of the lane, at the dark night sky, and back again to the spot on the ground where Ginny's bike had been found. "I don't know where she is, I have no idea. But I do know that she's nowhere around here. She can't be. They've looked. She'd have been found by now – hurt or concussed or lost, or anything. How far could she have got without the bike, and Maggie and Tracey finding it so fast, the wheel still bloody spinning?"

He paused. The police officer watched him resignedly. Violet was looking at the ground, at her feet. She couldn't work out what was worse – the robotic silence of before or this new and terrifying clarity, the certainty in her husband's voice.

"I saw such a wonderful future ahead for her," he said, his voice breaking. "No. Genette isn't here," said John. "I know that. She's gone."

"KEEP YOUR EYES OPEN"

August 21st, a Monday, followed another fruitless day of searching. There were still no leads, no fragments of clothing, no note discovered at home. *The Times* had picked up the story by now – *Bicycle in lane only clue to girl's disappearance* – describing the 150 police and neighbours who continued to search for Ginny. The article also introduced Detective Chief Superintendent Proven Sharpe, head of the Devon and Cornwall CID.

"Genette picked up the papers at about 3pm and rode off on her bicycle to deliver to farms just outside the village," he said. He described how she'd then met two friends, "stopped for a few minutes before cycling on, and leaving the other girls dawdling down the road for about 400 yards".

When she went missing, Genette had nothing with her except the clothing she had on. Money – savings for an upcoming family holiday – were also left behind. In addition, the money she'd collected on the round was found in her purse, which itself was discovered with the discarded bicycle. Clearly robbery was not a motive. In addition – and just as with April Fabb's disappearance – a hit-and-run-traffic accident could almost certainly be ruled out. No tyre marks were discovered on the road, and the bicycle, like April's, was found without a scratch on it. Any accident resulting in serious injury or worse would have left behind some evidence, however minute.

Proven Sharpe, the man in charge, had received the Queen's Police Medal in 1974 for his services to the force. For many years he had emerged as a shining example of good, honest police work in the South West; 1969, for example, saw an unprecedented number of serious crimes across Devon and Cornwall, including murder, rape and an attack on a police officer. Chief Constable Ronald Greenwood praised his officer for the successful investigation of these crimes, and Sharpe himself commented that "all the major inquiries into these major crimes were brought to a successful conclusion within the space of 72 hours". It was an impressive track record, and few could have doubted Sharpe's suitability for the gruelling task ahead of him following Ginny's disappearance.

The atmosphere at the Tate household was quiet that day, strained. John had spent all of Sunday and much of the night before wandering the fields, peering under bushes and tractors, stumbling down deep ditches and shining his torch-light into overground water pipes. Violet was glad to have him out of the house – it was amazing how quickly things deteriorated at home.

The bins overflowed with paper, notes, newspapers, cigarette packages, tin foil from all the many pies, quiches and pasta dishes they'd been brought. The ashtrays sat stinking in the front room, and the curtains were drawn tight over the windows. Ginny's bedroom had been picked through by detectives fresh from the fields who, though apologetic, had managed to tramp what seemed like half an acre's worth of mud up the stairs. The television set was firmly off.

In the sink, the cereal bowl sat under several newer, dirtier plates and cutlery, half-drunk cups of tea, a sugar bowl Violet had dropped and smashed yesterday. Just 48 hours before, the doors and windows had been open, the house was breezy and clean, the food in the fridge was fresh and the fruit in the bowl just purchased. Even their bedsheets now seemed filthy – they'd managed a little sleep, in the very early hours, but much of it dominated by restless tossing and turning, panicked dreams and sweaty, feverish brows.

He was there in bed now. John. It was eight o'clock, and he'd only returned home at three. She let him sleep and began to deal with the washing up, pausing only briefly before sluicing out Genette's cereal bowl, rinsing it and patting it dry again. She took the bins out and opened the back door, feeling immediately better, clearing the table of its pens, yesterday's newspaper, the switchboard number for Devon and Cornwall Police, the name of an officer assigned to speak with them whenever they required. Violet placed these items in the centre of the table and weighed them down with a rock from the garden, one of Ginny's, painted like a ladybird last summer.

She moved into the living room, transferring piles of clothes to a laundry basket, dusting the shelves and mantelpiece, and picking up the photograph albums that lay on the sofa. One was open – the most recent, it seemed. Violet sat for a moment, a cloth in one hand, turning the pages. She and John on their wedding day, beaming, the girls in the background. Tania on a donkey at the beach. Genette eating an ice cream at the zoo. Another day at the beach. A trip to South Devon to walk along the coastline, a camping holiday, a sports day at school, Ginny's embroidered PE top with her name across the shoulder.

For the past two days food had arrived sporadically on the doorstep, usually left without a note and without a knock on the door. They were grateful to be left alone. Occasionally someone tapped on the window, offering support and kind words, but Violet wished they wouldn't. It was becoming increasingly difficult to smile, to thank them. Now she couldn't stand it anymore. Let them see inside the living room: they could peek all they wanted.

She drew back the curtains and gasped. Outside, in the yard, four men stood or sat with cameras angled at Barton Farm Cottage. She saw one of them wave, an absurdly familiar, jovial sort of gesture. She jerked away from the window, shaking. What was happening here? Did the police not have the power to keep them away, these reporters and photographers or whoever they were?

She considered shutting the heavy curtain once more but decided against it. The house needed to breathe. She opened the windows, all of them, averting her gaze from the men outside. Sheila wasn't about to turn up and find the cottage a mess.

Ginny's mother had arrived in Aylesbeare the day before. She was gaunt with stress, her hair almost as wild as John's, and they'd embraced for a long time when the Tates went to collect her from the train station. She'd clasped Violet to her as well, sobbing, asking questions in between hiccoughs. It had all been too much, too intense. On Saturday, they could pretend that this nightmare might have a swift ending, that Ginny would make contact from Exeter or Birmingham or even London, that she would alert someone to her where-abouts, or that the hospital would phone to report a child matching her description who'd been brought in after an accident. Now, on the Sunday, it already felt a remote possibility, one that shrank with every passing minute.

Sheila had stayed in a local inn the night before, but today she was coming to the cottage. She wanted to sit in Ginny's room, she said, go through her belongings, search for a clue the others might have missed. The police had also suggested a press conference, an interview, and all three would be attending. They needed to speak privately beforehand.

At the time of Genette's disappearance, Violet was 36 years old, Sheila 34 and John 36. They were so young, all of them, to be dealing with this mess. And perhaps, as is so often the case at times of stress, their newly formed family unit was about to be tested in the most brutal of ways. Though Sheila was not Ginny's primary carer, she was still her mother. Now another woman had arrived on the scene to assume that responsibility – a woman who already had a daughter of her own. Perhaps, Violet thought, as she carried clean towels upstairs to the bathroom, Sheila would blame her. After all, had John not left Ginny to take her, Violet, to work on Saturday?

She paused at the top of the stairs and scolded herself. What a ridiculous idea. As if John would have gone with Ginny on the paper round. She'd been doing it long enough. She knew her way around. And hadn't Sheila congratulated her daughter on the job, not so very long ago? No. Sheila wouldn't blame her. Violet had done nothing wrong. The women had got on well when they'd met. Sheila and Violet had spent the evening out searching like the rest of them. And yet...

Again, she shook her head, refusing to let the thoughts take hold. Better to keep busy for now, she thought. Make it look reasonable here and you'll feel better. Not much to be done.

The idea of the press conference terrified her. All those clicking cameras and bright flashing lights. She'd seen other parents sit before the journalists, reading prepared statements, imploring their children to come home. She'd never understood how they'd done it. She felt, suddenly and very strongly, that she needed to have Tania close by. The rational side of her brain told her that it was better to have the girl elsewhere, away from all this, with her dad. But she wished it didn't have to be this way. The house felt so deathly quiet, so still.

Violet walked into the bathroom and began to apply her make-up. She combed her hair carefully and applied some scent. And then, steeling herself once more, she pushed open the door to her and John's bedroom.

"Sheila will be here soon," she said softly. John turned over, his eyes wide. God only knew how long he'd been awake.

Aylesbeare village hall was now serving as the hub of police operations. A team of officers was stationed there permanently, sifting through the ever-growing piles of statements, calls from the public and enquiries to be dealt with. Usually a place of community-led events – raffles, quiz nights, Girl Guides and Cub Scouts – it had taken on an eerie, focused atmosphere. Once again, Violet thought as they entered from a side door, it was unreal how quickly the familiar became terrifyingly strange. How swiftly their quiet village had been transformed into an efficient machine, and all for Ginny.

Sheila's arrival had been emotional, but not unpleasant. Violet found herself warming to the other woman, who complimented the furniture, the wallpaper, the neat borders of the garden. She had asked to look through Ginny's room alone and only then, on the landing, had they heard the faint sounds of crying inside. It was as if, from that moment, a switch had been flicked. Afterwards John, Sheila and Violet sat and talked without restraint, wept in turn, comforted one another.

John had managed to shave this morning and run a brush through his hair. He'd pulled on clean clothes, at last, and even made the pot of tea they'd sat drinking. His attitude was still one of silence, as closed off and unreadable as ever. But at least he was no longer lying in bed, glassy-eyed and frightening. Here he was, proactive, galvanised it seemed by the upcoming conference.

"They're taking it seriously, at least," he said, after his third cup of tea. "They want her found just as much as we do."

Sheila nodded, her eyes on a framed photograph on the mantelpiece. "Do they have a picture of her yet?" she asked.

"I've given them one, but I've been looking for something more recent," said John, gesturing to the albums now placed tidily under the coffee table. "Perhaps we can pick another before we go – the police said the papers will want it."

Sheila stood, smoothing down her skirt, and went to sit beside the table, turning the pages of the album slowly. "How is Tania?" she asked in a small voice, as Violet carried the tray of teacups and saucers through to the kitchen. "It's been some time since I saw her."

"Oh, she's alright," said Violet, grateful for the sincerity of the other woman's question. It was gracious – far too gracious – of Sheila to ask about Violet's daughter. "She's with her dad until we find Ginny."

That word – "until" – hung in the air between them, noticed but unremarked upon.

The three parents shuffled into view from the side of the village hall and were directed to a table set up at the back. This was now the marked-out "incident room" at the centre of all updates.

Before them sat an ever-growing crowd of reporters, many local and some national. August was a slow news month, meaning more than usual attended; in addition, a missing child in this part of the country was highly out of the ordinary.

"Thank you for coming," said John. He looked down at the notes before him. Under the table, Violet held his hand tightly. "Our daughter Genette was a normal, well-adjusted girl with no reason to run away." He cleared his throat, his voice catching. Sheila stared out at the photographers, her eyes taking on that glazed, faraway look Violet had come to know so well over the past days. "We are missing her enormously, and would like nothing more than to see her return home."

It must have been a scoop for the press. On either side of the eloquent Mr Tate sat both his former and current wives: the first a petite, high-cheek-boned woman with shoulder-length wavy brown hair and a floral shirt. Sheila glanced at Violet, with her neat shirt and trousers, her carefully brushed dark fringe and gently hooded eyes. They couldn't have looked more different either side of John, who was removing his glasses, clearing his throat again. The press snapped away, watching, taking in this most distressing of scenes. "We have no reason to believe she has run away," John continued. "And we've checked with others – her friends – who say the same."

A reporter raised their hand and waited for the sergeant to nod at him. "Sir, how can you be sure Genette hasn't run away?" he asked. "Were there any arguments between you, any rows?"

John looked straight back at the man. "Ours is a happy house," he said shortly.

"There were no family rows," said Violet, surprising herself. It seemed vital, suddenly, that these people got the full picture, that they understood. She'd heard of children slipping under the police radar when it was discovered they were from so-called "broken" homes, or if they were truanting, or generally considered to have been playing with trouble.

"We can't remember Genette losing her temper once." And as she said the words she realised how true they were. Ginny just wasn't the sort of girl to argue back, to make a scene, to throw a tantrum. She was a grown-up, really – mature in some ways but so naïve in others. She wouldn't, Violet knew, say boo to a goose. She was a polite child. Perhaps too polite. Perhaps she wouldn't have known danger when she saw it. Violet pushed the thought away and spoke again – "All we want is her back," she finished.

"We believe our daughter has been abducted," said John, and the cameras flashed. "She would not have run away, as we've explained. There were no issues at home, no reason for her to leave. Somebody must have seen her if that were the case, if she walked or cycled to the train station, bought a ticket, boarded a train. Nobody has come forward with this kind of sighting.

Ginny's bike was found in the middle of Withen Lane, its back wheel still spinning. The girls who found it heard nothing. Her newspapers were scattered over the road."

The policeman gestured at his wrist and Violet touched John's shoulder. Sheila coughed.

"She wouldn't fall for the 'sweeties' trick," she said. "She was intelligent and knew well enough not to do this." The cameras turned their lenses on Sheila, the other mother, the one who lived in a different town entirely, who wasn't even in Aylesbeare on the day Ginny went missing. As if sensing this potential reaction Sheila lifted her head high and stared back at the reporters. She gestured to John and Violet beside her.

"We've never quarrelled over Genette at all, and she comes to see me regularly."

John nodded. "Genette," he said. "If you're able to do anything off your own bat, then please telephone us, go to a policeman, or even write." The constable beside their table had lifted a hand to the remaining members of the press, the ones who seemed keen to continue the questioning. As they stood to leave the hall, John turned back to the scrum of cameras and notebooks, the clatter of chairs and hard rubber-soled shoes. "Please everyone," he said, "keep looking. Keep your eyes open – and don't give up hope." He was speaking as much to himself as the reporters.

The following day, Tuesday 22nd, police organised a reconstruction. Ginny's best friend, known only as Amanda X – her parents did not want her last name released – was tasked with the harrowing job of retracing Ginny's last-known movements.

Reconstructions are an invaluable policing resource. Memory is a funny thing, after all: fluid and prone to all sorts of mistakes, to forgetfulness. The brain receives many hundreds of thousands of messages per second, and must filter through them all to select the most efficient: the one, in short, that will keep the person alive. It will instruct us to zone out the noise of music, for instance, if we're doing something that requires a great deal of attention. It focuses on the task at hand, whatever that is, and manages somehow to block out the rest. All too often, witnesses to a crime simply don't know what might be useful, or even crucial, information.

Reconstructions can be vital to that unlocking, to the sudden realisation that on a particular day in a particular place, something the brain decided was irrelevant can be brought forward, remembered and used. If Ginny went missing today, it is likely police would still have employed reconstruction as a tool. Most recently, the high-profile case of Police Community Support Officer Julia James saw an actress walk her last-known movements across fields and through woods. Julia was discovered in April 2021 with significant head injuries while out walking her dog.

For many years, *Crimewatch* has been a forerunner in the use of televised reconstructions that may help police investigations – reaching a far wider audience than any locally staged appeal for information might allow for. These reconstructions begin with research, conversations with victims, investigating the person or people at the heart of any given crime. It is this proximity to the most horrific experiences that enables a high rate of viewer connection, and thus the ability to jog memories, recognise a potential witness or decide – often after many years – that their loyalty to another person may well be misplaced.

Ginny's case was particularly interesting in that, as today, police were well aware of the need for press attention. Newspapers were the most direct route into people's homes and therefore their knowledge of the missing girl, their ability to come forward with information, or the pricking of a guilty conscience.

Journalists were vital to cracking the case. The police's press officer, Roger Busby, was aware that "there was going to be some media interest" regardless of how much or how little investigators campaigned for Ginny's case. But the reconstruction was a part of the need to "generate" just such a necessary media presence. "The bike had been moved so we took it back to the scene and set it up as it would have been at the time Genette would have disappeared. Then we called a press conference to get as much interest as possible."

DS Rundle and DCS Sharpe knew they needed the help of the media. Exposure was crucial. On the very evening of Ginny's disappearance, Roger made a call to contacts in both the local and national press, letting them know that a conference would be taking place imminently.

It must have been a dreadful experience for Amanda, as she rode the short distance between the villages on Ginny's route. She was given clothes similar to those Ginny had been wearing, pushing the blue-and-white bike up Withen Lane, leaving it on the ground and stepping back uncertainly onto the bank.

Brian Hook is a lecturer in forensic sciences at the University of West London. Across the course of a 30-year career in the Metropolitan Police Service at New Scotland Yard he worked on over 25 murders, served on the Anti-Terrorism branch, the Major Investigations Teams and the Racial and Violent Crime Directorate. His professional life with the police bore witness to some of its most radical changes in procedure and crime-scene assessment and management. He was, in fact, covering his first murder inquiry in West London in 1978, the year Ginny went missing.

99

"What you have to remember," he says, "is that at the time we had 120 murders a year in the Met. Down in Devon that number was six. One of the biggest mistakes people, including police officers, make is assuming 20 years' experience counts for something as a detective. It's just not true if you're dealing with the theft of a lawnmower from a garden shed."

In the late 70s, local detective chief inspectors would ask for support from neighbouring stations and a certain number of investigators would arrive. While they might remain for a month or longer, eventually they'd return to central command. "There was no permanent core team, there was little continuity for those actually working major cases or any attempt to maintain a standard of knowledge," Brian remarks. "It's almost setting yourself up to fail." By this point, 120 officers were involved in the inquiry at Aylesbeare, and extra manpower was drafted in.

John Alderson, Chief Constable of Devon and Cornwall, claimed that the case represented "a complete mystery". The following day, the *Belfast Telegraph* described the "hundreds of people interviewed", the "fields and woodland combed". As each day passed, "many conventional lines of inquiry" were becoming "exhausted". A brief note at the end of the article alludes to the "several spiritualists and mediums" who, according to reporters, the police were now working with. This would come to have serious repercussions later.

On Wednesday 23rd August, the day after the reconstruction, a family came forward to say they had spotted a car in the vicinity on the afternoon of Ginny's disappearance.

Matilda Rogers, whose husband was a policeman in Hull, was on holiday in Aylesbeare that summer, along with her 14-year-old daughter Gail. They were renting a cottage on Withen Lane and reported seeing the three girls chatting just before Genette's disappearance.

As they crossed the little bridge over the stream where Maggie, Tracy and Ginny had met, walking away from the village centre, they witnessed a man in a car travelling in the same direction as the three schoolfriends. It was deep red or maroon, they thought. Later, under hypnosis, they would reveal more: the man, they felt, was likely to be in his 20s, dark-haired and handsome. The letters of the registration number contained an MB, or a BM, followed by another letter and numbers including 1. They were able to describe the interior of the car, remembered that the radio was on and even mentioned the colour of the driver's eyes.

The police were elated: these were the first credible eyewitnesses to the potential crime, and they seemed to be corroborated by another family, the Gormans, who, at the time of Ginny's disappearance, were travelling towards Aylesbeare from Exeter, where they lived. When they stopped at the village crossroads, they too spotted the maroon car, kicking up a cloud of dust as it went, and speeding back towards the city. No one had come forward to eliminate themselves from this particular line of inquiry, despite the fact the story was across all local and national news outlets. It was imperative the police gathered as much information as possible about this car and its owner. A silver-grey Minicar was ruled out of police investigations when it transpired the Gormans themselves had been driving it – indeed it was during this time that they spotted the maroon car.

Searches went on across the fields and ditches, hedgerows, gravel pits and hillocks surrounding Aylesbeare. Police frogmen donned their gear to sift through the summer algae of local ponds and wells, returning empty-handed. Investigators urged farmers to search their land, barns and outbuildings for any sign of Ginny, with one spokesman claiming it would take "an army of officers months to thoroughly search every inch of countryside in the area". The investigation moved, for a time, to a copse called Long Plantation on the outskirts of Aylesbeare, with 50 extra officers now going through this patch of land.

"Quite frankly, we need a break and fast," senior detectives claimed. It was four full days since Ginny's disappearance. Two local newspapers had offered rewards totalling £11,000 for any information leading directly to her safe return.

Inside the Tate household, life continued. Lunches and dinners were prepared, barely touched and thrown away. The fierce compulsion to search, so present in those immediate hours after the bike was discovered, had given way to a lethargy, a terrible gnawing ache. Ginny's pet cat, Mouser, had barely left the house since her disappearance: a farm animal with a great deal of freedom, he was used to roaming the lanes and fields all day, hunting. "We noticed that whenever we did anything," John recalled, "Mouser was with us. He was never very far away. It almost seemed at times that he was speaking to us." In addition, the Tates' dog Tammy, a spaniel cross, was similarly distressed. "She mooned about the place, wandering to and fro, never content. She was missing her daily walks with Genette. She was becoming deafer and her brown eyes were even sadder than usual."[8]What was there to do but wait? Every knock at the door, every tentative tap, gripped the three adults – John, Violet and Sheila – in a terrible panic. Surely this was it, the police visit they had been dreading. Something had been found, some vital clue. Someone had come forward with an indisputable eyewitness statement. Perhaps a local man had confessed to some hideous crime, and – while one set of officers was dispatched to Barton Farm Cottage to relay the news – a team was at that moment speeding towards an undisclosed location.

The press was not what it is now. There was no rolling-news coverage, no round-the-clock updates or social-media posts. The police were required to sift through information reported directly to them, or conveyed over the telephone. Any updates were given at press conferences. As a result, the public only had access to the facts that could be gained from the police, and as much as the newspapers were willing to report.

Nowadays, police must act especially fast to inform families when a key piece of evidence comes to light, when a vital clue is found, a "significant discovery". They must act to ensure the media is not able to broadcast the information before the family has heard it directly from the police. And, even more importantly, the scene itself – such as it is – must be preserved, free from contamination. While there were of course no Twitter feeds or WhatsApps to be concerned about in Ginny's case, news travels fast, especially in small villages. The police were aware that any finds of significance needed to be reported to Sheila, Violet and John without delay.

Searches led by Ginny's parents had focused on the route from the village hall to Exeter Airport. John had checked some of the old buildings en route, including a caravan. The sound of something moving over a sheet of galvanised iron brought them all to a halt, their ears straining for the sounds of footsteps, the hesitant approach of a teenager perhaps whose terrible practical joke had gone badly wrong.

"We decided it was probably a rabbit and made our way sadly back to the car and then home," said John Tate.[9]In the days leading up to August 30th, a local vicar – the Reverend Denis Large, who was rector of Aylesbeare – began making his own plans to help. The 60-year-old clergyman was deeply distressed by Genette's disappearance: he felt a certain amount of responsibility for the poor girl's family and the wider community, and in addition – perhaps correctly – he assumed that any potential abductor might well feel more comfortable getting in touch with him, rather than the police. Members of the tight-knit village were growing more and more disturbed by the day.

By this stage, police were in no doubt that Ginny had been abducted, and had not left of her own volition. There were a number of reasons for this. Missing children, especially those of Genette's age, often return home if they have decided to run away. The lack of evidence of any crash or accident confirmed the theory that police were dealing with an utterly random, opportunistic crime. No one could have known that Ginny had taken on a friend's paper route; still less would they have known the likely time that she was to deliver the newspapers, the route she would take, the time she'd be cycling back up Withen Lane, or whether she would – as was indeed the case – run into any of her friends on a bright day in the middle of the summer holidays.

Reverend Large decided to set up a 24-hour phone line, a day-long window of opportunity for the person or persons responsible for Ginny's disappearance to make themselves known to him. Small communities like Aylesbeare's, particularly in the 1970s, relied much more heavily on their parish priests, not only for spiritual guidance but as pillars of society, as emotional support, the eyes and ears of the entire population. It made sense, then, that Denis Large happened upon the idea.

The police were aware of the plan but played no part in its management or organisation – they were keen, however, to help Ginny's parents, and felt that the 24-hour timeframe might become well-publicised enough to provide some comfort. And if it resulted in a breakthrough, all the better. John, Sheila and Violet were unanimously in favour of the phone-in; John claimed, "It's just a matter of trying everything and anything."

All calls would be responded to confidentially, and Reverend Large implored callers to rest assured of their anonymity. He stressed the fact that any information would be passed to Ginny's parents, not directly to the police. "I do not want to know your name or where you are," he said.

"I only want to end the terrible strain and distress which Genette's parents are suffering. Just tell me Genette is still alive and give some proof that she is. If she is dead, phone me and tell me, if you can, where her body can be found."

With that, from Wednesday at noon until the following day, the rector promised to answer the phone. "If you telephone me, I shall answer. No one else will be listening. I promise that you will remain anonymous."

With that, Reverend Large went home to the Clyst St George rectory. The line – Topsham 3295 – was connected, and the vigil began.

Immediately the phone began to ring."Hello, Reverend." A man's voice, shaky and scared."Thank you for calling me. I hope I can be of some help.""I hope so too." There came the sound of ragged breathing, and then silence."Do you have any information for me today, sir? How can I help you?"Denis knew that a soft, gentle approach was needed. He was also terrified. It would be one thing to have no calls of any import, quite another to be told something hideous, to be confided in by someone who had committed an unspeakable crime. "I know where she is, Reverend," said the other man. "Genette?"

"Yes. She's still in Aylesbeare."The Reverend wrote this down, next to the current time. It was just after half past 12 in the afternoon. He signalled to his curate, working steadily on next week's sermon at the other end of the rectory's comfortable living room. The man picked up a separate notebook and held a pen ready."And you know this because you took her?""No, not me. But I know who did.""Well, for now, perhaps you could tell me where she is?""In the woods by the bridge. Right where the wee girls saw her before. She's in the bushes there.""Thank you." There was a pause. "Sir, can you tell me how you know this?"

The line went dead. Denis sighed, placed the receiver gently back in its cradle and ran his hands over his face. The curate looked at him questioningly.

"Not sure how much use that'll be," he said. "It was someone telling us she's by the stream, down on Withen Lane. I'll inform DS Sharpe, but the boys have looked everywhere round there a hundred times."

Over the next 24 hours, the phone barely stopped ringing. Reverend Large answered each and every single call, as his curate ferried cups of steaming coffee to and from the living room. At two o'clock in the morning a woman had rung in screaming, claiming that the forces of evil had spirited Ginny down to the underworld and that she, and only she, could get her out again. At 10 minutes past three, two giggling schoolboys rang – clearly kids on a sleepover, though God only knew where they were, or why they'd decided to ring and posit theories, wonder aloud where the girl had got to.

In an interview following the end of the vigil, Denis Large confirmed what he'd probably suspected from the start: that most callers were "very odd indeed. Many people kept ringing up for some extraordinary reason and then just hanging up. Other calls were more sinister. It makes me feel sick that people will ring in like this, knowing what the circumstances are."

He also discussed the many psychics, mediums and clair-voyants who'd made contact "with their own solutions, but unfortunately none were the same. I feel sure there is a person somewhere who is probably feeling terribly guilty and rather frightened about having done a terrible thing to a young girl.

When they do want to talk, they are going to say much more than Genette is alive or dead. That is why, I am sure, I have not had the call I am waiting for."

The next morning, local papers featured images of an exhausted-looking Large, a man who had tried so hard to provide Ginny's parents with the answers they craved, but who was unable to give anything concrete to the police. The vigil had ended without the results they'd all prayed for; the abductor had remained silent.

Dog walks, once an innocent feature of everyday life, had taken on a grim significance now for the Tates. If there was any animal bound to pick up her scent, it was Tammy the dog. John and Violet tramped the fields and hills, eyes darting as the spaniel leapt over fallen logs and sniffed through ditches.

On one of these walks, Tammy exhibited excitement and ran off, climbing uphill as the couple raced behind her, trying to keep up. She would turn on occasion, her tail wagging happily, and the Tates dared to hope. They'd not seen her like this for a long time.

As the going became steeper and they began to sweat, Violet suddenly stopped. "Look, John," she whispered. There, in a tiny clearing of brambles, was a pile of hazelnut shells. Beside it sat three sweet wrappers and a half-chewed ear of corn. John's hands shook as he surveyed the little scene. If anyone knew how to live off the land, it was Ginny. Was she out here still?

They continued to climb, following Tammy, until she stopped beneath a low-hanging branch. It all fell into place. A squirrel's nest – and a big one too. The animal was nowhere to be seen, now, but John was certain the discarded items they'd witnessed were nothing to do with his daughter. The squirrel had been foraging. And now the dog jumped up, her tail thumping a retort on the ground as she came back to earth.

"Down," said Violet wearily.

They continued, then, to the top of the hill. It was a bright day, clear and sunny. Tammy sat at their feet, licking her paws. In the distance forests of pine spread out before them like a thick carpet, lush and deep. One could see for miles around – the little thickets, the carefully ploughed fields, the untended meadows, the houses and outhouses, the little pinpricks on the horizon grazing on summer grass. It was a breath-taking view. But John and Violet Tate also knew, as they surveyed the land, that finding Genette somewhere within all that dense shrubbery, those thick forests and deep ditches, was becoming less and less likely. It was by nature wild, untamed, difficult to access, hard to traverse. Something might be lost here and never discovered.

"THERE'S BEEN A KILLING"

By Wednesday 6th September, Ginny's friends Maggie and Tracey had returned to school. The start of the new term represented a return to some sort of normality. It had been just a fortnight since the lives of the Tate family had changed beyond recognition, but what else was there to do?

"It has been a long and difficult summer for us all," said the headmaster. He looked around him at the pale, upturned faces, kids whose lives had changed completely over the space of just a few short weeks. "We will keep Genette in our prayers, of course. But we need to look ahead."

A pupil raised his hand near the back. "Sir, what's happened to her? Where is she?"

"We don't know," the man replied. It felt awful to have to admit it. "But if any of you have an idea of what could have happened, I urge you to come and speak to me about it. My door will remain open."

There was silence.

"And I would encourage all of you to be careful. Keep an eye on each other – walk with friends where possible. These lanes are quiet places, especially in winter. You know the rules about strangers already, but I will reiterate them. If you do find yourself walking alone and somebody approaches you, be on your guard. Most people will of course be harmless. But not all."

Schools around the local area and further away were advising their pupils to exercise caution. Nobody needed telling twice: the loss of Ginny had ripped her community apart, and its currents continued to be felt each new day.

While Maggie and Tracey arrived at their school gates once more, Royal Marines from the training centre at nearby Lympstone in Devon were called in to join the search. One hundred men arrived to walk the narrow lanes, scouring the fields and ditches, treading where so many before them had already walked. Ottery St Mary, a nearby town, was scoured as the men tramped through the dense fir plantations on the hillsides and along down the River Otter.

Two days later, it was reported that a local businessman had complained at the sight of shirtless police officers continuing to roam nearby farms and yards – the heat was punishing in uniform, especially for hours at a time. For whatever reason, the businessman had not heard the news about Ginny. Once he was informed, he himself went out to help.

Meanwhile the harvest was in full swing. All over the county farmers were clearing their barns, repairing combine harvesters and bringing in the corn from the vast fields that dotted the landscape. It had been a good summer: plentiful and healthy. But of course, the darkness persisted despite the long, warm days. DCS Rundle warned farmers to please keep a lookout for signs of Ginny as they tilled their fields – particularly, he warned them, keep a lookout in the blades of their machinery.

A fortnight after term had started, a Welsh woman called Pat Johnson raised the alarm after spotting a handwritten note on a road near the village of Corris, in Snowdonia. It was handed in to police, who alerted the Devon and Cornwall constabularies. "Help," it read. "I am a missing person. I have been captured in a car No HNO 244B. Please help me. I am frightened and want my mummy."

Police descended on the rugged Welsh mountains, speculating, hoping, wondering if this – the briefest of missives – might have been tossed from a moving car. Perhaps, after all this time, they'd been focusing on the wrong area entirely. Perhaps Ginny was already far from home, spirited away by person or persons unknown. The theory of her removal, accidentally or willingly, was now firmly established. There was nowhere in Aylesbeare left to search. And then, on September 20th, a 15-year-old girl from the Home Counties made contact with Scotland Yard.

Unfortunately, it was not the contact the police had hoped for. The girl confessed to writing the note herself while on holiday with her parents, and – on seeing the publicity her trick was generating – had admitted the prank had gone badly wrong. She had not meant to cause any harm, but now knew she had to come forward. Another series of days wasted, another round of inquiries for the police to close.

"It was the type of thing that could happen to anyone," said John Tate. "We were horrified to see the following day that some of the newspapers were condemning this little girl, when in fact we felt she deserved praise for coming forward so quickly... The police might have been involved in days of searching in the difficult terrain of the Welsh mountains where the note was found, if she had not acted so quickly and responsibly."[10] "It's a setback," said Violet Tate, "but we still feel Genette may be alive."

The "may" in her statement is telling. Police would likely have prepared the Tates for the worst as the days and weeks went on. Whatever hope they cherished could not, would not be extinguished unless police could say for sure that Ginny was dead. Nonetheless, the Tates were pragmatic. Ginny had only the money collected from that day's delivery of newspapers, and it was unlikely she could have got very far on that. Without any other obvious resources, how could any 13-year-old expect to survive in a city, especially one whose face was plastered over every village notice board and urban lamp post, a face many would recognise in an instant?

A week later, on September 28th, the hunt for Genette moved once more, this time to the grounds of a West Country estate called Castle Drogo. Members of the Dartmoor Rescue Group joined police, soldiers and tracker dogs to conduct a thorough search of the area, a popular tourist attraction. It stood over 20 miles from Aylesbeare. DC Eric Rundle – the second most senior detective on the case after Proven Sharpe – was keen to stress that these searches did not constitute any major new leads; nonetheless, "we cannot afford to discount any possibility." Nothing was found.

Miles away, other families began their own journeys down similar, terrible paths. On the Isle of Wight, Hampshire Police staged a reconstruction for missing 14-year-old Lorraine Herbert, who had last been seen on 5th September. Lorraine lived in Ryde and had vanished without trace.

And in a quiet, leafy district of south-east London, police were starting the search for another missing child, Mark Berkshire. On September 28th, the *Guardian* reported that the 11-year-old boy had gone missing from his school in Dulwich: Mark had only joined Kingsdale Academy three weeks prior to his disappearance. He hadn't had a happy start to secondary-school life and was teased – his family weren't wealthy, and reports suggested they may have been travellers, new to the area. He was bullied for his small size, for smelling bad, for never having his PE kit with him, and was dubbed the "Tom Thumb schoolboy" by the press. The last sighting of him was by an ice cream van parked outside the school at the end of the day on Monday 25th September.

"VOLUNTEER ARMY'S HEARTBREAK HUNT": on 2nd October 1978, the *Mirror* reported the search for the missing boy, which "ended in failure". Around 1,200 searchers scoured the streets and parks close to the school and surrounding area – the photograph shows a shy-looking, dimpled child with large teeth and a wide smile. Its caption: "still no trace".

Just four days later, it was reported that traders and businessmen from the City of London had offered £1,000 as a reward to help find Mark. A comment piece, again from the

Mirror, explains that "the problem of disappearing children isn't new", referencing both April and Ginny and quoting Scotland Yard, who issued the following advice to parents:

"Communicate with your kids. Know where they are going. Know who their friends are. Tell them never to go out with strangers. Tell them why and tell them what to do if they are approached by strangers." The comment piece concluded with the opinion that "keeping children in ignorance of the dangers doesn't help to keep them safe".

"Please Mark," said his mother Pat, in a television broadcast which aired on Thursday 26th October. "Get in touch with me." It was later revealed that a neighbour had been receiving hundreds of prank messages after Mrs Berkshire provided her telephone number for any information relating to Mark's disappearance. The neighbour, who lived in Trust Walk, between Tulse Hill and West Dulwich, had been asked to take down the messages on Mark's family's behalf – they didn't own a phone.

Weeks went by without information or leads. Two months after Mark's disappearance, however, a small body was discovered in undergrowth in a shallow grave at All Saint's Church, on Rosendale Road. The body was later confirmed to be Mark's, and it was estimated that he was murdered not long after going missing.

Later, a 16-year-old boy would be found guilty of his murder in what was described as "a game gone wrong". Very little information exists about Mark's case, despite the length of time between his disappearance and the recovery of his body. The news, however, reached Aylesbeare. John and Violet Tate sent a message to Mark's family after he was found: "We are thinking of you," they wrote, asking the media to "tell them how sad we are".

On October 22nd, the two sets of parents met, with Pat and Brian Berkshire travelling down to Devon. "Our day-to-day lives were worlds apart," recalled John, "but we were drawn together by a bond of grief and found a tremendous amount of comfort in each other's company. For the first time we really felt that someone knew what they were saying when they said to us 'We know how you must feel.'"

Yet another case was dominating the headlines at the time, and once again it involved a child on a paper round. Carl Bridgewater was Genette's age when he stopped at Yew Tree Farm, near Stourbridge in the West Midlands. Inside lived two elderly pensioners, Mary Poole, 79, and her cousin, Fred Jones, 76. Ordinarily – if the door of the farmhouse was open – he would hand the newspaper to them directly.

A month to the day after Ginny's disappearance, the door was indeed open. Carl called inside to let the pair know he had arrived, but nobody answered his calls. It's unclear exactly what transpired next, but it is generally accepted that Carl interrupted a burglary taking place at the exact moment he arrived. He was shot in the head at close range, most likely to prevent him identifying the men responsible.

Four men became of interest to police, including two cousins, Vincent and Michael Hickey, James Robinson and Patrick Molloy. There had been a spate of violent armed robberies in the local area recently: in late November 1978, a Tesco super-market in Birmingham was held up at gunpoint while the safe was raided; just a few days later, another elderly couple were threatened with a shotgun at Chapel Farm, in Romsley.

Carl Bridgewater was described as a cheerful child, an active Boy Scout who lived in the village of Wordsey. His father, Brian, stood on the doorstep of the terraced house and spoke to the press shortly after it became clear the so-called Bridgewater Four were responsible for his son's death. His wife, he said, was at the time in bed under sedation.

"These men are ruthless. They have no thought for other people at all," he said. "I just hope that anyone who is harbouring these killers comes forward with information, because these people are sadistic. If anyone could just come forward and give information to the police, this is all I ask. I know the police are doing all they can. We must leave it in their hands to sort out, but I am a very bitter man."

The four men were eventually arrested and found guilty of the crime, but their convictions were quashed in February 1997. It transpired that Molloy, who died just three years after the attacks, had made a false confession.

A month after the Bridgewater Four's conviction, a local man named Hubert Spencer used a sawn-off shotgun to shoot dead another elderly local man, Hubert Wilkes, who lived just a few hundred yards from where Carl was killed and who, like Carl, was left for dead on the sofa at his home. Whilst in prison, Spencer, a former ambulance serviceman, admitted to another inmate that he had shot Carl Bridgewater. It transpired that Spencer had been interested in the antiques owned by the couple at Yew Tree Farm and, knowing that Carl – who lived two doors down from him – could identify him when he was disturbed mid-robbery, he'd decided to act. To this day, Spencer denies the allegations made against him, and claims the confession was fabricated.

The tragedy of another stolen life, another fathomless crime, shook a nation still reeling from the terrifying events unfolding in Devon. Although the circumstances were different in many ways, it seemed once again to confirm the fear that the country's children were unsafe: a previously innocent, wholesome way of life was being transformed. Perhaps, parents reasoned, it was safer to keep their children close.

Nine weeks after Ginny's disappearance, the police were out of ideas. There were no new leads – and those they did have had taken them nowhere. It seemed impossible for a child to simply vanish without trace, but this was what they were faced with. The past month had witnessed a flurry of new leads, all investigated, and all in vain.

If Ginny had been abducted, as was assumed, the motive was certainly a sinister one. Statistics proved that when paedophiles snatched children, they were unlikely to be found alive. This dreadful prospect would have haunted the Tates as they continued their search. Nonetheless, with nothing fresh, the police operation began to scale back.

Newspapers require information – they need the momentum of clues, of something uncovered, a rumour even.

With Genette Tate there was nothing, and over time – slowly, like sand running through an hourglass – her story began to fade from public consciousness. As is so often the case, it was the people of Aylesbeare, the villagers left behind, who were preparing to reckon with an uncertain future and with a new way of life, one where children were ferried inside quickly and doors shut firmly behind them. They discussed it among themselves, but now the conversations were tinged with sadness, with regret. The panic and energy of those initial days and weeks was being replaced with an awful sort of acceptance. Perhaps they would simply never know.

After around five or six weeks, the police turned to their last resort. Now the clairvoyants and paranormal experts were consulted, the soothsayers and psychics. Indeed, it was on the advice of one such medium that Castle Drogo had proved the focus of fresh investigations in mid-September. In December 1978, *The Times* reported that 200 people had returned to the East Plantation, a mile from Aylesbeare, to comb for clues. As John Tate returned home from work each day, he saw groups of officers digging where expert tracker dogs had alerted them to potential remains in the ground. It must have been a dreadful sight.

Like Reverend Large before them, a group of psychics had organised another phone-in appealing for fresh leads, this one led by a television scriptwriter called Andrew Wilson. The plantation, he claimed, was chosen as it was reported to have "good vibrations", while a "major European clairvoyant who is seldom wrong" had also indicated the area's likely involvement in Ginny's case. "We were not looking for a body," he was quoted as saying, "but for mystical clues". By this stage, police and volunteers had already searched the plantation twice, moving in tight shoulder-to-shoulder lines and stopping every time an object was discovered and investigated. The undergrowth and tall thickets snatched at clothes and bare skin; Sheila, Ginny's mother, returned home covered in scratches.

A clairvoyant from Bexleyheath called Nella Jones had advised the group to search for a piece of cloth: a blue strip of fabric was duly found during the group's search, and henceforth sent off for expert examination.

For the police, any available source of information becomes understandably important after a certain amount of time. If there was any way to shed new light on the case, it seems they were open to it. And who can blame them?

Psychics may seem laughable nowadays, but many would be surprised just how often – and how relatively recently – their testimony has been acted upon. Although they cannot be used as reliable witnesses in court, many contemporary cases have seen their involvement in one form or another. It is often the parents or family members of missing persons who make contact with mediums themselves, rather than the other way around; most would hesitate to contact grieving families directly.

In the summer of 2002, almost a quarter of a century after Ginny's disappearance, the UK was gripped by another missing-child case – this time in a sleepy village in

Cambridgeshire. Just as Ginny's school photograph captured the public imagination, imprinting her toothy smile forever more on anyone old enough to remember it, so the poignant image of Holly Wells and Jessica Chapman, two 10-year-old girls in matching Manchester United tops, would go on to mark one of the biggest manhunts in UK police history.

The parents of Holly Wells accepted the offer of help from a medium, in the dreadful fortnight-long period between their disappearance and the recovery of their bodies. Dennis McKenzie, a 48-year-old clairvoyant from Cambridge, arrived at the Wells family home at their invitation.

Like Ginny's disappearance, there were few leads in the days immediately following Holly and her friend Jessica's fateful trip on a warm Sunday afternoon to buy sweets. They were not seen or heard from again, and although several members of the public – along with CCTV cameras – had spotted them walking down a local street together, there was no way of knowing what happened to them afterwards.

Dennis began his interview with the Wells family by asking how they would like to receive any information. There were two options: the first was complete, unadulterated truth; the second a more positive inference of any negative messages received. On Wednesday 7 August, three days after the girls had vanished from their Cambridgeshire town, Dennis delivered a terrible blow: "I am really sorry," he told Holly's parents, "but both the girls are dead."[11] He went on to provide the following information to the distraught parents: first, that there were three people involved in their daughter's death, two men and one woman. He claimed that one of the men, who had dark hair, was in his mid-30s, while the woman, who looked "quite young", had "mouse-like features". They were not, Dennis claimed, "from this area", describing their northern accents as "possibly from York or Manchester". He went on to describe the perpetrators' car, an older red model, and suggested the children had been "wrapped in something, possibly bubble wrap, but likely carpet". He also informed the Wells family that "the girls have been moved away from Soham". He claimed that the letters C and O were within the address of the property.

"Kevin," he said to Holly's father, "you've walked past this house while you were searching."[12]Almost two weeks to the day after the girls went missing, police discovered the children's missing Manchester United T-shirts in a bin on the grounds of the local Soham Village College. These bright red tops became synonymous with the investigation as the girls were photographed wearing them, happy and smiling at a family barbeque, just 90 minutes before their deaths. The day after the discovery, a dogwalker in nearby Lakenheath made a frantic call to police. The moment nobody ever wanted had arrived, and the girls' bodies were formally identified the next day. Both had been badly burned and dumped in a ditch; they were in a dreadful state of decomposition.

News quickly broke that Ian Huntley, the school caretaker, had been taken in for questioning alongside his girlfriend, Maxine Carr. Huntley, who was from the north of England and in his mid-20s at the time, had appeared on televised interviews at the start of the investigation as the last person to see the girls alive. He claimed he'd noticed them on August 4th as they returned from buying sweets, and they'd had a few minutes' conversation. He and Carr – a classroom assistant at Holly and Jessica's school – lived together on College Close, though Carr had been away visiting her mother on the night the girls vanished.

Police did not involve Dennis McKenzie directly in their operations, yet Kevin Wells – Holly's father – set a fair amount of store in McKenzie's revelations, noting the physical descriptions of Huntley and Carr; the fact he, Kevin, had apparently walked past the house where the girls were reported to have died many times during his searches; and the fact they were not local to Soham. Huntley's house was located on College Close, an address with two Cs and two Os.

Detectives in Ginny's case were not prepared to rule out any line of inquiry. As the weeks dragged on, it became imperative to use every resource available, no matter what they thought about spirituality.

The difficulty lies in the fact that every phone call, piece of unsubstantiated rumour or gossip, a sudden remembrance of one thing or another – all has to be logged, traced, examined. The man or woman claiming to be a psychic medium might indeed be the abductor, the thief, the murderer. In 2006, a group called UK Sceptics asked every police force in the UK if they'd ever used a psychic; all but one gave a categorical negative, except for the Met. It seemed police had not always been sceptical about employing the help of those who claim to have knowledge of some ethereal "other side".

In 2015, the College of Policing published new guidelines for its officers searching for missing persons, and advised – perhaps to the force and wider public's surprise – that information from those purporting to be psychic should not be dismissed. Officers were urged to check the "accredited success" of any such "witches and clairvoyants".

The document states that high-profile missing person investigations "nearly always attract the interest of psychics and others… stating that they possess extrasensory perception. Any information received from psychics should be evaluated in the context of the case and should never become a distraction to the overall investigation and search strategy unless it can be verified." Incredibly, in 2007 the Ministry of Defence was found to have spent £18,000 on experiments designed to test psychic powers.

It stands to reason, perhaps, that whether or not the psychics approaching the teams searching for Ginny were of any material use or not, they were at least helping to keep the story alive in the press, especially during the long winter months, when the tragedies of Carl and Mark were so firmly in the public eye.

By the end of 1978 the police had been contacted by no fewer than 100 mediums and parapsychologists, each with their own theory as to Ginny's whereabouts and what had happened to her. These "dowsers" would stand with sticks hovering over maps, attempting to indicate where she might be. One man even posited the theory that Ginny had been abducted by a UFO and taken by spacecraft to Venus. During John Tate's own phone vigil, he described being "pestered every half hour by a man who insisted that Genette was in a caravan on the main Sidmouth Road... I was later to learn that this man had obtained his information by swinging a pendulum alternately over his Jack Russell terrier and an Ordnance Survey map of the area."[13] On Friday October 27th, yet another less-than-conventional avenue was opened as a possibility. The *Mirror* reported that a hypnotist had been enlisted to help jog the memories of key witnesses. Maggie and Tracey, the children who'd discovered Ginny's bike, were put into a trance and subsequently "able to give details which were used by an artist to do an oil painting".

John Tate, who was also placed under hypnosis, recalled these attempts to unlock some buried memory, describing them as "a load of rubbish". One can imagine the grim, ghoulish scene as the girls sat and allowed themselves to be lulled into a trance-like state, a state that might enable the recollection of some previously buried detail.

In many ways this is not in itself a bad idea. The brain naturally focuses on relevant stimuli – a sudden noise, the phone ringing, the fire alarm, the ping of a microwave – and filters out that which it classifies as irrelevant. This is referred to as "sensory gating" – the neural process of ensuring only the most relevant information reaches the brain.

The 1960s and 70s had seen a huge rise in interest in all things paranormal, psychic and extra-terrestrial. Uri Geller, the Israeli-British magician and illusionist, made a name for himself through various psychokinetic feats – he bent spoons, made watches stop or run faster, and ascribed his powers to the strength of willpower and telepathy. The moon landings had increased a hungry public's belief that literally anything was possible, that there was life beyond what could be seen or imagined.

Mike Charleston, a reporter with the *Daily Express*, discussed the possibility of keeping an open mind with DCS Sharpe. The police and press were, it seemed, working together: they decided between themselves that the time had come for another approach.

The *Express and Echo* newspaper had reported the police's use of less conventional search methods just four days into the investigation. *Devon spiritualist leads inquiries to village pond* ran the headline. Chief Constable John Alderson announced that a medium had been tasked with aiding investigations: "Yesterday a spiritualist from Exmouth came to the village. He said he was getting some feelings about Genette being in the water – in this case a pond. As we are taking notice of all leads we organised a search of the pond by divers but found nothing."

Gerard Croiset was what might be considered somewhat of a celebrity by this point: he had worked closely with the police on April Fabb's disappearance over 10 years earlier. His methods included studying maps of the local area before allowing intuition to guide him to the missing person's where-abouts. "The man with the X-ray eyes" was duly requested to join police on their hunt for clues relating to Ginny's disappearance. "My secret," he said, "is to think in pictures while other people think in words."

Croiset had become a household name over the past decade. He assisted police in their searches for the victims of Ian Brady and Myra Hindley, the notorious Moors Murderers, and predicted the location of Lesley Ann Downey's body.

Croiset set off by car alongside the reporter, Mike Charleston, and police officers, travelling the roads in and around Aylesbeare. There was silence as they watched from the windows, the fields and skeletal trees whizzing by. The place looked entirely different from the photographs taken at the scene after Ginny's bike was discovered. It was winter now. They imagined the snow and ice covering hard ground, the things it might be concealing.

"Stop the car," said Croiset suddenly. They skidded to a halt outside an old quarry on Woodbury Common, an area of heathland around four miles south of Aylesbeare. "There's been a killing."

"This is it," Mike remembers thinking. They exited the car and followed Croiset. The season was turning, the first signs of spring just tentatively starting to appear. Soon the lanes would be covered in slowly decaying leaves, littered with conkers. Ordinarily the children of Aylesbeare would be out collecting them – but not this year.

Mike stood a little behind Croiset as the man looked around him, closed his eyes and rotated slowly on the spot. The tension was palpable. He reached down and touched the ground, running his hands over the thinning grass.

The Dutchman paused. "Yes, there will be a killing..." he muttered. Mike gaped at him. Croiset rose. "Not now," he said, "in the future."

The men stared as one. It was hardly the information they were so desperate to receive. Croiset paused again before shaking his head. There was nothing more to say.

Police could hardly act on reports of a crime not yet committed, and so the drive resumed. Croiset felt nothing else.

Ultimately these tip-offs came to nothing. By January of 1979, the Tates were reconciling themselves to a landscape of life without their daughter, without closure. Police kept them regularly updated, but life was moving on. Crimes such as this simply didn't happen in Aylesbeare, but they certainly did in neighbouring towns and cities, and it wasn't right to focus the majority of their resources on one case, no matter how tragic. And so it was that the operation to find Ginny, the 13-year-old papergirl with the flares and blue-and-white bike, was slowly scaled back.

John Tate never gave up hope that his daughter might one day be discovered. Indeed, it seems incredible – given the passage of time, the development of infrastructure and the careful, patient searches for human remains – that she has not yet been.

The years after Ginny's disappearance were not kind to John Tate. For many months after the local and national news crews had left, he continued to search across the narrow lanes of Aylesbeare, looking for clues other searchers or the police might have missed, eyes alert for a scrap of clothing that seasonal weather changes might have dislodged. He sat beside a phone line similar to that of the Reverend Large, waiting for a call that might provide some sort of solution. Perhaps, if the perpetrator didn't want to speak with a member of the clergy, they'd speak to the child's father himself.

As the years passed and his health began to fail, John Tate moved north, to Manchester. After all this time, the constant daily reminders had proved too much – markers of the streets and lanes Ginny had once walked then cycled across, the school she'd attended, the slowly emerging adulthood of the friends she'd had. The lives of Maggie and Tracey had continued apace: as the weeks turned to months they grew up, became young women, moved away, developed lives of their own.

His new existence, away from friends and neighbours in Aylesbeare, seemed now to revolve around his daughter and maintaining public interest in finding her. He gave anniversary interviews, followed up on subsequent leads – often travelling the length and breadth of the country to do so, and once even to Europe, when someone matching Ginny's description was spotted – and wrote two books about his daughter and the search to find her.

"We made the mistake of allowing Genette to do a paper round," he wrote, "something she was happy doing. At the time when she asked to do it, we could only see the benefits: the fresh air and exercise, and something to keep her occupied and out of mischief. We did not see the pitfalls."[14] It is hard to imagine many parents seeing the pitfalls of a child riding her bicycle in late-1970s rural Devon. But, as John himself stated, the event "brought home to us with a bang that we are living in much more violent times than we had appreciated."[15]It seems cruel that his final years robbed him of the mobility, and therefore the opportunity, to continue the search for Genette himself. He needed round-the-clock care following a major stroke and was confined to a wheelchair; he was also suffering from McArdle's disease, prostate cancer and diabetes.

In his last major interview, two years prior to his death, John stated that it was his dying wish "to know where Ginny is. Just to know that she has been found and given a Christian burial would be enough. There is no closure... I suppose I just don't want to accept she is dead... If we could just find her body that would give me the proof I need."

Someone knew what had happened to his daughter, just as someone knew what had happened to April, Christine and Mary. The not knowing, the possibility – however slim – that she might be alive would prove a constant torture. They say ignorance is bliss, but it can also be a curse.

Two years after Ginny's disappearance, Gerard Croiset died in Utrecht in July 1980, at the age of 71. His insights into the case did not, ultimately, move the investigation forward. The fact that the police were willing to try, however, speaks volumes about the willingness, the intense desire to crack the case.

It is a desire that continues to this day. Genette Tate will be remembered across the country by those who followed the story as the 1970s ended and the 80s began. It remains one of the UK's biggest mysteries.

Part Three:

HOLMES

THE "RIGHT" VICTIM

When detectives made contact with local and national press in August 1978, their cries for exposure were answered. Reporters from the *Western Morning News*, the BBC and the Press Association assembled on Sunday morning, the 20th, to begin their coverage of the missing 13-year-old.

"So, they found the bike," said one cameraman, climbing out of the car, "but nothing else?"

"Not a sausage," said his colleague, who'd arrived an hour earlier. "No signs of a struggle. Bike was in good nick – no dents or marks."

"And you'd think a kid'd be so safe round here," said the cameraman sadly. "Took me hours to find it – never even heard of the place before this morning."

He began to snap away at the surrounding countryside, at the police combing the hedges, at the village hall's flurry of activity.

Poignantly, the *Exeter Express and Echo* – the newspaper Ginny had been delivering when she disappeared – placed her picture on its front page. During the reconstruction, the girl's bike was laid on its side in Withen Lane, in the exact spot it was found, and papers were scattered across the road, just as Maggie and Tracey had described.

The image was to become the defining symbol not only of Genette Tate herself, but of a changing attitude to the freedoms young people were losing, a sense of childhood interrupted, an end of innocence.

By Monday morning, Richard Lappas – a photographer for a local agency called Devon News – claimed that "the whole world and his uncle were in Devon. All the London staff people came down, there were dozens and dozens and dozens... Newspapers, magazines, TV and radio. Aylesbeare was under siege."

Anyone who recalls the disappearance of Genette Tate will remember that photograph of her bike on its side. As a visual representation of unsolved crime, it was perfect in media terms. Here was a quiet, idyllic country lane in the middle of the English countryside in summer. When the girls discovered the bicycle, they reported that its rear wheel was still spinning. In the weeks and months following Ginny's disappearance, this fact lodged in the minds of adults and children alike.

"Fancy it happening that quickly," said a woman to her husband. They'd helped join the search all day and were now at home, discussing the day's events in the kitchen. "How long does a bike wheel spin for, anyway? Ten seconds? Twenty at most?"

Her husband raised his finger to his lips, pointing. Behind the kitchen door the couple could make out two pairs of motionless feet: their children, eavesdropping.

Maggie Heavey had been moments, perhaps mere seconds, away from the crime that nobody seemed able to solve. Whatever had happened had been quick, efficient, brutal – more so due to the silence, the lack of screams or cries for help. How often she'd wondered, in the weeks since, whether she and Tracey might have helped. If only they'd walked with Ginny instead of reading the newspaper. She knew they weren't to blame – everyone had said so – but still the guilt weighed heavily. In her quieter moments, usually late at night, she allowed her mind to consider the other, dreadful possibility – that if she and Tracey had accompanied their friend, they too might now be missing and presumed dead.

Reconstructions had played their part in the media circus. Here were two schoolfriends peering at the discovered bike, the newspapers across the ground, the bright August sunshine of what should have been a perfectly ordinary day.

When it comes to criminal cases, what does or doesn't capture the public imagination can be hard to pin down. After the Second World War, the victims of crime themselves became much more prominent in legal proceedings and, consequently, in the media. The primary victims – those who experienced any number of incidents ranging from robbery to arson, fraud to sexual assault or bodily harm – were given much greater focus than had been the case previously, when most reporting focused on the perpetrator.

Increasingly, the secondary victims of crime – in the case of murder, for instance, the victim's family – were likewise pushed front and centre of emerging news stories and were often used for press appeals, victim-support statements if the case reached a trial stage, and – particularly over the past 20 years – first-hand accounts of the impact the crime had not only on them, but on their wider family and community. Books written by such victims offer a compelling insight into their unspeakable stress and pain.

Sarah Payne lived with her family in Hersham, Surrey, but was visiting her grandparents in West Sussex on the evening she disappeared. She had been playing with her two brothers and younger sister on the late afternoon of July 1st, 2000, when she was snatched from the edge of a cornfield by convicted paedophile Roy Whiting. Seventeen days later, her body was discovered in a field 15 miles from where she had been taken. Michael and Sara, the little girl's parents, were instrumental in leading the press charge as the country held its breath, waiting for news and praying for a positive outcome. Eight-year-old Sarah was Roy Whiting's victim, but as the days and weeks unfolded, the public's sympathy focused equally on her family, on the parents and siblings she left behind, and the irreparable damage caused by her murder.

The majority of crimes dealt with by police are not reported by the media. These are the financial or legal disputes, corporate cases, tax-evasion files, low-level, petty burglary and theft, muggings and internet crime ranging from hacking to identity theft. Crimes such as these, however depressing, happen every day. Whatever destruction is caused, the fact remains that the crimes themselves are not extraordinary.

We know, too, that many thousands of children are reported missing every day, but only a small handful of such cases occupy column inches in a newspaper, and of these, it's easy to spot a recurring trope.

What's clear is that press attention for Genette Tate's case was high. It faded, as time went on and leads dried up. There was little fuel to add to the fire of the case – with no evidence, fresh leads or new eyewitness sightings, attention moved elsewhere.

A case is usually classified as "cold" after a year or so, often placed on hold until such time as information comes to light or a new team arrives to re-examine the evidence.

We can compare the response to Ginny's disappearance to that of April Fabb's, Christine Markham's and Mary Boyle's. Mention their names to those old enough to remember and it is Genette who rings a bell, albeit dimly. The others were largely forgotten by the media as the years went by, and any press that was generated – such as in the case of Mary Boyle – was often the result of updates from the secondary victims, the family and friends left behind after the crime, the disputes that form in its terrible wake, the anniversaries and birthdays causing fresh pain or new memories.

The Tates' meeting with Pat and Brian Berkshire, Mark's parents, had revealed the differences between the two cases. "Although police methods were good in both places, some aspects were better in one area than in the other," recalled John Tate.[16]"For example, our police public relations office here had been very good. They had organised police press conferences, where we were taken along to meet all the press in one go. In Pat's case she had had journalists knocking at the door continuously. We realised that we had received a tremendous amount of coverage in the press and on television in comparison to the meagre amount that Pat had received." John stated that the "circumstances surrounding Mark's disappearance were just as mysterious as those concerning Genette. They had just as little idea of where Mark was as we had of where Genette was. In stark contrast, only two clairvoyants had offered to help Pat and only one medium wrote to her."[17]When a case is high-profile from the outset, the chances of securing a conviction tend to be higher. We have seen in the cases of Sarah Payne, Holly Wells, Jessica Chapman and Milly Dowler, as well as the recent tragic murder of Sarah Everard, that a combination of police work, public awareness created by the media and pressure to secure convictions has resulted in what secondary victims might call justice. The appalling racially motivated murders of Stephen Lawrence and Damilola Taylor were also solved due to a combination of the factors above.

And yet the reporting of such cases seems to be the exception to the rule. Despite a county-wide manhunt for Christine Markham's abductor, news of the search didn't extend for long into national headlines. Mary Boyle's case was stamped on the minds and hearts of Donegal residents for years to come, and on Ireland more generally – but few people in England have heard of her. April Fabb's case was obscured by Ginny's, her name gradually fading into obscurity. And even Ginny herself was soon consigned to the back pages, only emerging as her father continued to keep the press on-side.

The list of missing children who have not yet been returned to their families is a long one, but most people will never have heard their names. And one reason for this is the public perception of victimhood itself, of what makes an "ideal" victim.

It helps first to look at the reverse. To understand what constitutes the ideal victim, we need first to understand the typical one.

In surveys conducted on the subject, a few key criteria emerge: criteria that suggest a lack of surprise, and therefore a lessening of empathy, on the part of the public when certain members of society suffer crime of any sort.

The typical victim is young, generally male, almost always working class. He will usually live in an urban environment. If such stories do hit the headlines, and they rarely do, images and facts are accompanied by tell-tale indicators. The pre-teen or adolescent boy may have what's so commonly called "a troubled background". He is likely to come from a "broken" home, usually a single-parent family. He may have a history of playing truant, or even a criminal record, a previous caution for shoplifting or assault, vandalism or antisocial behaviour. When such a boy goes missing, it's assumed that he's run away, or that his lifestyle – whatever form that took – has somehow contributed to his disappearance.

On an early Boxing Day morning in 1996, two such boys left their homes in Chelmsley Wood, a housing estate in Solihull. Patrick Warren was 11 and David Spencer 13; Patrick left home on his brand-new red Apollo bicycle, a Christmas present, and David left on foot.

Birmingham is a huge city, the second largest in the UK. Like London, Liverpool and Coventry, it suffered enormous damage during the Second World War, and the decades afterwards were spent rebuilding, redeveloping. In the 1980s its economy had all but collapsed, and unemployment rose drastically. The Chelmsley Wood estate was built in the late 1960s with the aim of rehoming families already on the council-house waiting list. It was huge and sprawling, easy to lose oneself inside. It had a bad reputation. In 1991, the sole mention of it in the national press is from one Mrs McMulkin, who required "newsboys/girls" promising "excellent rates of pay" who were prepared to deliver in the afternoons only.

David Spencer had red hair, brown eyes and stood at around four foot seven. He had recently been expelled from Coleshill Heath School, marking his exclusion from mainstream education, and had more than once been obliged to attend the local youth court. More often than not, playground disputes had ended in fights and David, not one to shy away from such action, was usually, as his teachers reported, in the midst of them. He was a keen boxer. Patrick, just two years younger, was about three inches taller than his friend. He had blondish hair and light eyes, loved playing football and had a good sense of humour.

Both children had spent Christmas Day outside, playing in the snow.

"Boys," called the warden on duty that day, in Meriden Park, "stay off the frozen pond, ok? You'll fall straight through. Dead in seconds. I've seen it happen."

The boys giggled. The groundsman moved off, shaking his head. They stayed for a little longer, playing and chatting, and then returned home to David's house. They made plans to visit one of Patrick's brothers together, and set off.

They never arrived.

Back at the Warren household there were five other siblings to worry about, crammed into a tiny flat. It was a cold, frosty night. In neighbouring towns and villages across the country, other boys their age slept soundly in their beds.

As Christmas Day ended and Boxing Day began, the boys visited a Shell garage and were given a packet of biscuits by the attendant, who remembered them heading in the direction of the local shopping centre.

When another of Patrick's brothers, Derek Warren, found out the following morning that the boys had never arrived at his brother's, he raised the alarm. Some weeks later, Patrick's bike would be discovered behind the garage.

Although the case was treated as a missing-persons inquiry from the start, there was no urgency to the police's reaction. Senior officers posited, in veiled terms, that there was nothing to suggest they had come to any harm. And although local press picked up the story for a time, reports tended to focus on David as a "streetwise" child who knew his way around.

It was assumed that no harm could come to these children, and that they would – when they were ready – return home to their families of their own accord.

Four months later, prompted by similar missing-children's cases in the United States, Patrick and David's photographs were the first to be printed onto milk cartons in the UK. It was a novelty, a strange new phenomenon, but despite the fact that many thousands of people across the country would see the boys' faces as a result, no information was forthcoming.

The campaign to raise awareness in such a way was launched by the National Missing Persons Helpline in April 1997. It is likely that any recollections pertaining to that chilly Christmas night were long forgotten – and very few people were out and about as it was. There is no more silent night than Christmas, after all.

Patrick came from a large Irish family; his mother Bridget later reported that, when she lost her temper, he'd tease her about her strong accent. "He was a bit on the wild side," she said in 1997. "There's no point saying he was an angel, because he wasn't. I would say he was cheeky. But other kids' mothers used to say, 'Paddy is a terrific little lad'; even his teachers said he was a good lad."

David's mother Christine described her son as "adorable, a lovely lad". She was under no illusions that David could nonetheless be "aggressive" – "he didn't like discipline," she said, "you couldn't tell him what to do... If someone caused him grief he took the law into his own hands and used force to keep them off his back, which was unacceptable."

The case of the "Milk Carton Kids", as they came to be known, has never been solved. The boys weren't seen or heard from again. A criminologist later studied the police response to David and Patrick's disappearance, and concluded that their background and socio-economic status directly impacted how the case was overseen.

"If it had been two boys from [middle-class] Solihull that went missing, that case would've been treated initially very differently," said Professor David Wilson. "And it's about that word we're never allowed to use, class – this was about a class judgement that was made which was prepared to see them as runaways, as opposed to vulnerable."[18]

Five days after the boys went missing, a 17-year-old girl called Nicola Dixon was preparing for a night out on New Year's Eve. The rest of the Dixon family were away for the evening, visiting relatives in Northumberland; their daughter remained behind in the West Midlands to take her driving test, which was cancelled due to the snow. It had been an especially cold few days.

The A-level student attended Fairfax School where she studied art and photography; she was described as bright, hard-working and popular, "with a wide circle of friends". She lived in the Royal Town of Sutton Coldfield, just 10 miles north of Chelmsley Wood, David and Patrick's estate. The area was affluent, had minimal levels of poverty by comparison and some of the most expensive homes in the West Midlands area.

Nicola went missing after leaving a party at the local social club, Good Hope Hospital. When she left at 9.45pm on New Year's Eve, her intention was to meet another friend at the station pub near the town centre. She was dressed to impress, that night, in a leopard-print blouse, black trousers and a leather jacket. She cut down an alleyway close to Trinity Parish Church on her way.

At 10am the following morning, as the country awoke with sleepy half-formed resolutions for the new year, the wife of a local rector discovered Nicola's lifeless body in the grounds of Trinity Church, outside the unoccupied curate's house. She was found with serious head injuries. Forensic evidence revealed she had put up a fight, despite her slim size – she had tried to climb over a gate and escape.

The attack had occurred just a mile from her home. Nicola had been raped before her killer smashed her head against the kerb. Her father, a 53-year-old civil engineer, spoke to the press some years later and described the events surrounding his daughter's death. "It was very out of character for her not to have called us as promised that night," said Andy Dixon. "She'd never done anything like that before. But there are 101 reasons why kids might not call, or go home when they say they are going to, and you can invent far more plausible reasons than what actually happened. Yet what actually happened is the one you worry most about as a parent."

Police scoured the land for anything that might aid the investigation and conducted over 11,000 interviews, gathered 6,000 statements and, in an appeal for witnesses, provided

BBC's *Crimewatch* with information for a programme dedicated to the case. In addition, almost 3,000 people in the area had their DNA tested – a novel and fast-growing means of identifying culprits beyond reasonable doubt.

Nicola's killer had his DNA taken just seven months after her murder, when he broke the jaw of his then-girlfriend and was convicted for assault, serving four and a half years in prison. He was released in 2001, and in August 2002 was once again arrested for attacking a motorist in a road-rage incident. When another DNA test was taken, it matched evidence found at the Dixon crime scene. West Midlands Police later claimed that a problem with the packaging of the original DNA sample meant it was never sent to a forensics lab for testing. Nonetheless, the case ushered in new practices requiring all prisoners to submit DNA as a matter of course.

When Nicola's killer – an opportunistic employee at the local Cadbury's factory – was arrested, the court heard that the chances of the DNA found at the scene belonging to anyone besides Colin Waite were a billion to one. The jury deliberated for just under half an hour before finding the defendant guilty, and Waite was jailed for life.

Nicola's case dominated the news headlines in the days following her murder. Her killer was caught and convicted, and justice would have been served much more swiftly had the original DNA been processed. In addition, her murder brought about positive change which doubtless contributed to the resolution of other serious crimes.

But while her death sent shockwaves around the country, some residents from Chelmsley Wood, just 10 miles away, had never heard of the Milk Carton Kids.

The two cases – Nicola Dixon versus Patrick Warren and David Spencer – can be viewed alongside one another. Nicola was middle-class, female, well-educated with a good school record and that all-important "bright future". Her parents made direct appeals to a press keen to listen, providing childhood photographs of a blonde toddler in a red skirt, matching red shoes and white ankle socks. Her killer was arrested, tried and convicted.

There were few current photos of Patrick and David; they were working-class from a notorious estate in a deprived area of town, with less-than-adequate school records.

Their disappearance was not given the same degree of attention by either the press or, it seems, by the police. A former teacher at Coleshill Heath recalled David as a bright child who "had quite a presence", commenting on his "unpredictability – you couldn't tell with him when something was going to go wrong". The teacher went on to express "surprise" when David wasn't found. "That was one of the things that always puzzled us – he was one of the most streetwise pupils we had at the time."

2021 marked the 25th anniversary of the boys' disappearance, a grim milestone marked by a community who claimed authorities had not acted with sufficient speed to find the children. David's brother, Lee O'Toole, was just nine when the crime took place, and he has spent the past quarter century attempting to discover what became of the boys. Accusing West Midlands police of negligence, he decided to instigate a dig focused on an area of interest in Solihull. "The community is doing what the police should do," he said.

Despite frequent reports from a local who reported seeing a man digging on or around the time of the boys' disappearance, "police have never acted on it," said Lee. "They've left me no choice other than to put the shovel in the ground."

The differences between those regarded as typical victims and ideal victims is stark. If a missing adult is educated, hard-working, married, middle-class and white, it is much more likely that their case will attract publicity. On the reverse side, the damning indictment of a "high-risk" or "itinerant" lifestyle, a previous record of arrest or time served in prison, often belies a sense that the person's disappearance is somehow to be expected. And even if a victim is generally found to be "ideal", there is no guarantee of fair reporting or investigation if she also happened to be "on a night out", wearing "revealing clothing" or intoxicated.

But of course, there's no such thing as the "perfect" victim after all. And yet media reporting of victims tends to focus on this unattainable state. Watch any true-crime documentary and spot the references to the "perfect couple", the fact the victim had "everything to live for" and was expected to achieve great things. But what of the ordinary lives? The victims who just had futures, pure and simple, ahead of them? Futures filled with washing up, savings accounts, holes in tights, toast and Sunday morning lie-ins?

There's a sense that stories become newsworthy if and only if the victim can be presented as close to perfect as humanly possible; there's something almost fetishistic in the reporting of "high-society" murders, acts of criminal violence against the rich or well-connected – how the mighty have fallen, readers are led to believe.

The disappearance of Hannah Williams in April 2001 caused little media outcry. Hannah was working-class and had been raised by a single mother; she'd run away before. Across the course of her disappearance and the eventual discovery of her body, just 60 articles were produced on the case, and most of these came after her body was found. In its first two weeks alone, the hunt for Holly Wells and Jessica Chapman generated some 900 articles in the British and overseas press. Hannah went missing at the same time as another girl of similar age, Danielle Jones, and indeed around the same time as Milly Dowler. When Hannah's body was found, it was assumed to be Danielle's. The only difference between Hannah, Milly and Danielle, really, was their backgrounds – two of them produced a perfect "ideal victim" narrative and the other became "deserving".

Chris Greer, criminology professor at City University in London, has written extensively on this subject. He suggests that while some victims are automatically granted this status, others must work to achieve it.

The murder of Stephen Lawrence was just such a case. Police initially dismissed the brutal slaying as gang-related, believing that since Lawrence and his friend were black, this was the only possible explanation. It was the campaigning work of Lawrence's family and friends that began to paint a different narrative. Suddenly here was a boy hoping to become an architect, studying at two different colleges for qualifications in physics, technology and English language and literature. During his teenage years, Lawrence, a keen and devoted runner, had competed for his local athletics club,. Somehow, that transformed the image of Lawrence and made people sit up: despite the apparent barriers of skin colour and the fact he lived in a working-class district of south-east London, Lawrence's education and character helped his image to migrate from "typical" to "ideal" victim.

While officers were informed of the perpetrators' identity within days of Stephen's murder – messages were left on police-car windscreens identifying the men responsible – no move to arrest them was made. It was a fortnight before any arrests were made at all, and the five people responsible were subsequently released without charge.

Black victims of crime are far more likely to be portrayed as living in unsafe environments, increasing the likelihood of assumptions that they brought the crime (whatever it is) on themselves. Like migrant workers, sex workers or those with otherwise "high-risk" lifestyles, the pressure on police to solve crimes against these demographics is lower, simply because the public has been led to believe that crime amongst these communities is to be anticipated.

The most easily identifiable victims, then, are those understood from the beginning to be innocent, vulnerable and without sufficient experience, strength or understanding of a dangerous criminal situation to defend themselves. On the spectrum of "perfect" to "typical" victims, children and the elderly – especially women – rank highly on the former, while young men, addicts and the homeless are regarded as somehow less worthy of compassion. As Professor Greer writes, there exists a "hierarchy of victimisation" which is "reflected and reinforced in media and official discourses".[19] The publicly held view of the "ideal" victim – however subconsciously it is held – was challenged in January 2006 by the-then Metropolitan Police Commissioner, Sir Ian Blair. During a discussion on wider police investigations at a meeting of the Met Police Authority, he came under fire for suggesting that "almost nobody" could understand why the Soham murders became "the biggest story in Britain". He later apologised, suggesting he had not intended "to diminish the significance of this dreadful crime" but to heighten the difference of reporting when it came to news value. The notion of anyone challenging victim status in this way – especially someone as well-respected in the industry as Blair – shocked the public.

One of the key issues is not only how much coverage a victim receives at the time of the crime perpetrated against them, but how much that coverage continues, and how often it's repeated. Without doubt, repeated appeals for information on anniversaries or following the release of new information, a memoir or anything else pertaining to the case in question, keeps it in people's minds, and ensures that the perpetrator is more likely to be apprehended – even years later.

In addition, news agencies are only as intelligent as the people who work in them. It's a bit like artificial intelligence, which can perform insofar as its creators have programmed it. We hear, then, about racist robots, about air bags in cars designed specifically with the average height and weight of a man as their model. If news agencies are predominantly made up of white, middle-class journalists – as they almost all were during the 1960s, 70s and 80s – then their focus will invariably home in on those most like them. As gatekeepers of the information received by the public, it falls to families and friends of victims outside this demographic to campaign on behalf of their missing or murdered friend. If news agencies believe that the public is more interested in a certain type of victim than another, they will of course feature that victim again and again.

But if the profile of an ideal victim can be established – as it holds the most fascination for the public – then it also stands to reason that the ideal offender can be profiled too.

MISPERS, DATA-SHARING AND PROFILING

Petra Pazsitka was 24 when she failed to arrive at her brother's birthday party in Braunschweig, Germany, in 1984. She'd recently submitted her thesis and was last seen leaving the dentist. Her family were bewildered: she'd given no indication that she was planning to leave. She was reported missing and an intensive search was launched; after her case was featured a year later on a popular German television show, a man came forward to confess to her murder. In later years, he would retract this confession, however, and no body was ever recovered.

Five years later the cold-case file was officially closed. It was 1989 and the Berlin Wall had just come down. Petra's family gave up hope of seeing their daughter alive again and resigned themselves to a life of not knowing.

That was until September 2015, when police responded to a woman's report of a burglary in Düsseldorf. Although the woman identified herself as a Mrs Schneider, she could provide no identification bearing that name, and on further questioning confessed to stunned officers that she was, in fact, the missing Petra Pazsitka. When pressed, she produced an out-of-date identity card to prove it.

For the past 30 years she had been living anonymously in various German cities; she had no passport, driver's licence or bank account and paid all bills by cash. Her family was astonished at the news: it had long been assumed that Petra was dead, that her killer was walking free. While her father had passed away several years before, her mother and brother were desperate to meet with her, to have that long-awaited reunion. And yet Petra refused. They passed on a letter through the police, just in case. Still she refused. And despite the frustrations of a police force keen to see a solution to the case – in addition to the efforts, resources and time given over to it immediately after her disappearance – no crime had been committed, so they were powerless.

As in Germany, anyone over the age of 18 in the UK has the right to go missing. It's not a crime. Police have a duty to establish that a missing person is alive and well; once this has been completed the case is closed, and they are legally bound from disclosing where the person in question currently is, or forcing them to return home. If appeals have been made online, police are obliged to remove these once a safety check – in person – has been performed. This doesn't stop a missing-person case appearing in other online spheres, of course, but the "right to be forgotten" is enshrined in law, and people can request any personal information relating to them to be removed. They are, in short, entitled to their desire – however incomprehensible – to start again, to go off grid and stay there.

There are exceptions, of course. Children do not have the legal right to go missing. And if a person is considered to be a danger to themselves or others, they can be sectioned under the Mental Health Act. The police's current "misper" (missing persons report) guidelines have specific sections, too, devoted to missing individuals with dementia.

Merlin is an online catalogue of the vulnerable utilised by the police. Any time they or social services interact with a vulnerable member of society, records are updated. Merlin will reveal the history of a person or reports on their welfare. A misper will remain on the system even when an individual is found, to show that a person has been missing at some prior point.

Policy guidance issued as recently as April 2021 outlines investigation protocol for basic-command-unit inspectors and sergeants. The guidance is clear – "most missing adults and children are not located by police but return home of their own volition after varying periods of time."

So what might police set in motion once a missing person call arrives in 2022? The avenues are comprehensive and wide-reaching, from the basics – obtaining via email a good-quality recent photograph – to the more in-depth, like examining social-media presence, updates or a sudden ceasing of such updates. CCTV, the guidance suggests, is "underused in most cases", while "last known direction/ location/clothing worn/appearance/in company with/ timings" are all vital and "can provide significant updates and investigative leads".Similarly, officers are advised to make use of "eyes and ears on the street" such as parking and community wardens and neighbours, locals, those with the same daily routine. Officers are advised to speak with the missing person's friends or associates because "if we establish lifestyle we can decide what is or is not out of character". Financial checks include debit-card usage, large withdrawals or – just as telling – non-usage. Police are also asked to check whether a person has previously gone missing, to "clarify the circumstances and last placed located", and to consider looked-after children, "likely to gravitate back to family or previous locations".

Most important, it seems, is the history of a missing person: "if we establish lifestyle, we can decide what is or is not out of character". And here's where victim behaviour comes in.

When a person goes missing nowadays, their level of risk is graded, like a triage system in a hospital. "Someone just missing could be late home or present significant concern dependent on individual circumstances."In the cases of April, Christine, Mary and Ginny, their missing episodes were certainly out of character. They were all under 18 and in good physical health, without known mental-health issues. Then, as now, police acted quickly – guidelines suggest the "immediate deployment of police resources when the risk of serious harm is assessed as very likely". Once it had been established that the four children were indeed missing, presumed abducted, those resources were deployed.

But hands were tied in the 1960s and 70s. There was a great deal stacked against police in the hunt for the person or persons responsible.

Most violent offenders are known to their victims. These are the crimes committed in the heat of the moment – the ex-boyfriends or jealous husbands, for instance, who may have, until fairly recently, seen lesser charges brought when accused of murder. In 1707, the English Lord Chief Justice described a man having sex with another man's wife as "the highest invasion of property" and stated the aggrieved husband "cannot receive a higher provocation". Although the defence was abolished in the UK in 2010, the notion of a "loss of control" still exists, which has seen murder charges reduced to manslaughter in similar, modern instances. In these cases, the killer is usually caught red-handed, or turns himself in to police of his own volition.

Violent crimes committed by strangers are rare. They usually occur as a result of another crime's discovery – such as waking up, hearing a noise and finding a burglar, then killing them out of self-defence, fear or anger. Or vice versa. The burglar is terrified of being identified and facing a lengthy prison sentence, so attempts to eliminate the witness.

The most incomprehensible – and the most chilling – violent crimes are thankfully the least common. These are the planned attacks on strangers, for whatever reason, and involve careful planning, weeks of watching and the securing of alibis. If juries find "a significant degree of planning or premeditation" has occurred, this is known as an aggravating factor – it makes the offence more serious.

What was startling about the crimes committed against April, Christine, Mary and Ginny was that no premeditation appeared to have taken place. Long before any possible link between them had been established, their abductions seemed completely random – no forethought could have been given to their disappearances, because it would require an impossible degree of knowledge. Mary Boyle and Genette Tate were actually deviating from their usual routine when abducted – Ginny through the shift cover of the paper round, and Mary because she was only staying with her grandparents for a short period of time.

What could police have made of the crimes? All victims were girls between seven and thirteen. All were white. All were outdoors, alone, when taken. Three of the four were taken from rural areas on roads that were ordinarily quiet, unbroken stretches, some distance from the main motorways. Whoever had taken them had acted impulsively, had travelled away from the main streets, had managed to carry out the abduction without alerting witnesses, and had transported them elsewhere. Such random kidnappings suggested either extreme intelligence or incredible recklessness: someone confident but simultaneously out of control. Any one of these victims may have resisted enough to break free and run.

Who was the perpetrator?

Lawrence Byford was frustrated. He scanned the documents littering his desk and sighed. The clock on the wall continued its slow tick. The rest of the house was silent, its inhabitants long gone up to bed. It was November 1981, well past midnight, but this was when Byford worked best.

The reports laid out before him made for sombre reading. By his calculation, a total of 1,021,489 hours had been spent searching for the man the press had dubbed the Yorkshire Ripper. The investigation into the murder of the poor Rytka girl – Helen, just 18 – had involved almost 200,000 hours alone.[20]Peter Sutcliffe, for now they knew his name, had terrorised West Yorkshire for the past six years. In that time, he'd murdered 13 women across the county and in Greater Manchester. Police had spent some £4 million trying to catch him, gathered around a quarter of a million statements and checked 5.2 million vehicles. And then the man had been brought in entirely by chance in early 1981.

On 2nd January, Sutcliffe was arrested for driving with false number plates. Inside the car the bewildered officer on duty discovered a knife and a hammer and, two days later, their owner confessed to his many dreadful crimes.

Lawrence Byford, the Chief Inspector of Constabulary, had been tasked with understanding what had happened. He'd risen quickly through the ranks after joining the force in 1947; three decades later he was awarded the Queen's Police Medal and was made a CBE in 1979. Three years later, Byford would be knighted.

A five-year reign of terror, and all those mountains of paperwork, had done nothing to bring Sutcliffe's murders to a halt. Byford was putting together a comprehensive review of police operations during that time; the report was due in three days. He sighed, turning the pages, sipping the coffee which had long grown cold. It was ironic, he smiled to himself, to be sat here surrounded by exactly what had so hampered the police in the Sutcliffe saga. Everywhere he looked folders teetered on side tables, jostled for space among boxes of files and facts, figures, endless reams of paper. Witness statements, logbooks, memos, action plans. The delivery men had carted it all in over the space of two hours. His study, once so meticulous, looked like the hiding place of some deranged fanatic. Bloody paper everywhere. A sea of it, mountains of it.

In real terms, Byford knew that paperwork had been almost as deadly as Sutcliffe himself. This had been one of the 20th century's biggest police operations in the UK. How was it that all those officers, all those detectives, all that time, had achieved so little? They'd taken 30,000 statements across endless house-to-house enquiries and 250,000 "persons seen" actions.

With this staggering amount of information at their fingertips, how could the killer – for investigators were sure they were looking for one man – have slipped through the cracks for so long? It seemed as though police had every hope of apprehending him: the sheer volume of information was astonishing.

Over the past months, it had become apparent that what the forces involved lacked was efficiency and organisation. All information was stored on handwritten index cards, cards which were then actioned slowly in what became a bottleneck at the main incident room at Millgarth Police Station in Leeds. When new information was ready for review it was passed from one pair of hands to the next, then waited in wire baskets for the next relevant officer to sift through the batch. The teams were overworked and exhausted: the press demanded answers to which they could only respond that they were doing their best. And the bodies continued to pile up. Lives snatched off the streets, lives cut brutally short for no apparent reason. They'd be working away on the circumstances surrounding one death when the dreaded phone call came in to announce the discovery of another. It was endless. Thirteen women. Thirteen lives snuffed out.

Byford was dealing with "the letter" as the clock struck one. Outside, the wind whistled through the garden, lightly rattling the panes. The darkness was complete; no lights shone in the distance and his reflection alone was visible in the soft glow cast by the table lamp. He wondered what it had been like for those women. How frightened they must have been. They'd known the danger, after the first attacks revealed Sutcliffe's pattern of victims, but necessity – money, food, rent – had driven them out into the wet and cold.

Byford knew what that was like. They'd had no money growing up either. He'd joined his father in the coal mines of West Yorkshire when he left school without a single qualification. The pits were awful, dirty and claustrophobic, but it was a job. He couldn't work out, some 40 years later, whether that had been worse than his next employment, conscripted in 1944 and posted across to France, Belgium and Germany. It all seemed such a long time ago now.

He continued; the steady clicks of typewriter keys filling the air once more. The letter in question had caused police a great deal of hassle. It had arrived at the incident room a year before, in November 1980, and the writer claimed to have "every good reason to believe" he knew "the man you are looking for." It was "only recently", he said, "that something came to my notice, and now a lot of things fit into place. I can only tell you one to two things which fit: for example, this man has had dealings with prostitutes and always had a thing about them. Also he is a long distance lorry driver." The writer provided a name and address and asked police to "check up on dates" as they "may find something". The name of the man in question was Peter Sutcliffe.

When the letter arrived, it was – of course – one of many. Byford remembered some of his earlier cases, the telephone calls and long, meandering notes they received which all had to be logged, acted upon. He knew the Sutcliffe teams were inundated. And the public were desperate to help; in fact the police had appealed for their aid, and reward sums only continued to grow.

Byford scanned the sheets of paper pertaining to the letter. When it was received, it was marked "action to trace/ interview Sutcliffe" by a detective sergeant and marked as "Priority Number 1", meaning actioning the information would be simple since the writer had provided "good detail": a name, address and credible motive. Priority 2 or 3 might include much more vague or even nonsensical detail – "my neighbour did it", "my friend goes for long walks at night" and the like. Fine. That was good. Byford nodded as he read, then groaned.

"That incident room," he muttered, "has a lot to answer for." The typewriter keys clicked faster.

Before the advent of Holmes, which replicated the card system in electronic form, all missing persons and murder inquiries would begin with an index of people. The victim in question would be "Nominal 1": white cards that lived in their own carousel and around whom everyone and everything else revolved. The Nominal 1 card gave details of the victim, their appearance, age, address, family, education. Dates of birth went on a separate carousel, a green spinning wheel of names and dates. Statements were numbered and logged under other nominal cards – witnesses, friends, associates. A separate index would list addresses containing the number of occupants in a particular property. In short, to find the necessary information, an officer might need to wade through the information on six or seven cards, in different locations, before finding what was required. It was a paper chase best suited to help solve minor incidents rather than complex, spiralling abduction or murder cases. And it all relied on humans – flawed, tired, hungry, dispirited perhaps – to ensure standardisation.

On this occasion, as Byford read, a policewoman had prepared an action form for Sutcliffe to be traced. This form was then passed to an index clerk, who was tasked with creating a new card for the subject of the letter – in this case Peter Sutcliffe. She also needed to check and see if there were other index cards related to Sutcliffe. She found three, and summarised their findings on another new card. This process took some 10 days to complete. She then placed the action card in one of the wire filing baskets, enabling the old index cards to be copied and attached to the new action card, and then the whole thing would be sent to the outside inquiry team. Byford's head hurt just reading it.

For whatever reason, the file remained in the wire basket, actions waiting to be actioned, and Christmas came and went. Nothing happened.

Byford stared at the dates between the letter's receipt and the next action. Ten days. Ten days in which the man could have struck again. Just imagine if he had.

What were they doing? He considered it all, staring once more out of the shadowy window. He could imagine the scene. Five long years and nothing to show. People moving sluggishly, dutifully following the leads but without any urgency. He typed his next words slowly, deliberately: "General malaise".

So much work had been done, and crucially so much filing, that even the most able clerks seemed to have become lost in a desert without a map. The papers that needed copying on this occasion were filed in a separate room many were unfamiliar with and may not have known how to locate. "They weren't trained," he said. "No one knew how to use the system, so the system failed. They avoided the stuff they didn't know, the stuff they'd never been taught." He tapped his fingers on the desk.

"Because of this unfamiliar procedure, it would seem," Byford wrote, "such work naturally gravitated to the bottom of the filing basket." The letter's valuable information had sat, gathering dust, while station officers scrambled their dwindling reserves of energy.

Byford flicked through the interview records once more. Following his arrest, it became apparent that Peter Sutcliffe had been brought in for questioning on nine separate occasions. Nine. He shook his head. It was like finding a key piece of a jigsaw puzzle, a particularly tricky section of the map or image, and then instead of placing it among the others like it, simply tossing it in the bin. The paper used to record these interviews, the index cards detailing Sutcliffe's previous interest to police – none of it was easily cross-referenced. No one could doubt the police's efforts when it came to time and dedication to catching the killer – but without the right tools, they were groping in the dark.

What they hadn't bargained on was the amount of information they received, and their inability to log, store and categorise it. What made things even more difficult was the speed with which one crime followed another – the murders were being documented and investigated even as another tragedy unfolded, another body discovered.

Byford pulled the incident room photographs towards him. At one stage, its floor was actually reinforced – it was starting to creak under the weight of all that paper. And every time the police appealed for information across this spate of 13 separate crimes, they received still more information, more leads, names, addresses, actions to follow up.

"Couldn't see the wood for the trees," he said to himself slowly. "How anyone could have waded through all that's beyond me." The clock struck half past one. He needed to finish up.

The Ripper incident room ought to have been the effective nerve centre of the whole police operation, he typed, but instead it became a serious handicap to the investigation. The backlog of unprocessed information resulted in failure to connect vital pieces of related information. He didn't like writing it, but it was true. The serious fault in the central index system allowed Peter Sutcliffe to continually slip through the net.

Any organisation is only as good as its filing system, its methods of administration. You can have the brightest team, the most hard-working senior management, but without a way to document and record tasks as they are completed or followed-up or discarded, it's impossible to progress. Admin, though long regarded as dull and formulaic, can be the difference between life and death.

This was the task facing police in the 1980s: while evidence-detection, interview techniques and science had advanced, the system of collating it all had not. On their side were incredible new methods, like DNA, that would no doubt see conviction rates soar, but only with the right tools. There was little use in making progress in a major inquiry if that progress was recorded manually. The system relied on humans, on handwriting and diligence and thoughtfulness. One absent-minded recollection could have enormous consequences. A teetering pile of index cards and folders could see the crucial one fall under the table, spill open, slip behind the filing cabinet.

What they needed was a master filing cabinet – an electronic one.

In 1985 the system known as Holmes – the Home Office Large Major Enquiry System, named after Arthur Conan Doyle's great detective – was formally launched. Its intention was to collate information when major, large-scale enquiries ran the risk of a paper-trail overload, a system designed to increase efficiency and serve as a weapon in the police's armoury. It could also store information on missing persons, casualties, survivors and evacuees – making identification and next-of-kin notification much more streamlined.

"The first time I ever had hands on a computer was in the Holmes classroom," Brian Hook recalls. "It was 1989 and I'd been selected to go to the anti-terrorism branch. Before me was a green computer screen with a little flashing cursor – there was no mouse, and to move it we had to use the up, down and across buttons." Brian's three-week course was designed to teach police how to use Holmes, how to interrogate it, how to log on and input a name and search through pre-added indexes. "It's probably the biggest stem change investigative-wise," he says, "It was a huge leap, a magnificent tool."

The original Holmes encompassed three different versions of one system and was not rolled out across every force in the country. It was the first, the prototype, and as such it had various weaknesses that needed ironing out. The police had all the information, often enough, but the computer system wasn't advanced enough to know what to do with it or how to link it.

It took some four years to establish and around £35 million to update the original. Holmes 2, as it was known, could link all the forces via an internal portal, an information web that could be accessed by any officer at any time. This computer was able to read hundreds of thousands of pieces of information as one document.

Instead of relying on its human modellers to make the connection, the computer itself could now suggest links that might otherwise not have been made. This system of "diagramming" is able to build networks between various connections, from phone numbers to lifestyle habits, locations visited or previous convictions. Back in 2000, when the IT-service company Unisys launched Holmes 2, it was made clear that the technology could only work with what it was given: if individual forces refused to release information onto the system, then of course there would be glaring gaps in its diagramming capabilities. "The technology is willing," said Unisys's Doug Stuckey, "but the culture is weak."

Since 2004 all forces in the UK use Holmes – enabling them to link incidents, share information or conduct joint investigations. It is a uniquely organised system with various sub-headings, from forensic submissions to house-to-house enquiries, interviews, electronic messages and transmissions, questionnaires and statements. It is most useful in serious crime where the identity of the offender is not known.

Thankfully, it's a lot more difficult to escape detection in the 21st century. The difficulty was re-examining old, cold cases using the new methods available. But cold cases have a bad rap within the force as a whole. Conviction rates are low, and the chance of success therefore minimal. The fresher the wound, the easier it is to establish what has caused it. An age-old scar might not provide any real information whatsoever; too much time has passed.

Detectives naturally want the fast pace of modern, contemporary crime – crime which has a decent chance of being solved. And the colder a case becomes, the less likely it is that families, the media or other advocates will put pressure on officers for a solution. Like a snake eating its own tail there's nothing to stop the cycle, and the mystery stays on the dusty top shelf, where people largely ignore it.

STOW

Stow is a tiny village south of Edinburgh, close to the border between Scotland and England. With a population of just under 800, it's cut through by the Gala Water, a tributary of the River Tweed. Nearby, the grassy Moorfoot Hills provide a pretty backdrop to this ancient place with its bridge dating back to 1654, its low parapets intended to allow the safe passage of horses.

There are several theories about the naming of Gala Water. Some suggest it's derived from the Old English *galga*, or gallows, while others claim it comes from *gal*, a word in Brittonic, the ancient Celtic language, meaning enmity or hatred. According to legend, Stow was once the scene of King Arthur's victory over the Saxons, leading to his founding of the first church in the area; dedicated to the Virgin Mary, it was apparently endowed with fragments of the True Cross.

It's a quiet place, historic and serene. Tall stone houses complete with mini turrets stand proud against the only wide road in the village, while woods of tall trees canopy the smaller lanes. The busy A7, the Galashiels road, cuts through the village, neatly bisecting one side from another.

It was 1990: 31 years since April's disappearance, 18 since Christine's, 13 since Mary's and 12 since Ginny's. These were now old, cold cases. Nobody spoke about the girls anymore – not the media, nor the officers once assigned to their cases. Some of them had retired, moved away, even died. Only the girls' families held out hope that their bodies, at least, would one day be returned.

In the meantime the world was changing: how different it would have looked now, how much more advanced. Children of the 60s were fully grown themselves, perhaps with kids of their own. The news had moved on.

The summer of 1990 was long and hot. All across the UK the mercury was climbing and showed no signs of stopping. In Scotland, however, the mood had been sombre. Just two years before, in a town just 60 miles from Stow, a scheduled Pan Am flight departed from Heathrow Airport, bound for New York City. There were 259 passengers and crew on board, the majority of whom were American. The journey began in Frankfurt, included London as a stopover and was due to stop in New York before finally connecting to Detroit.

Just 40 minutes into the flight, at 7.03pm on 21st December 1988, the Boeing 747 exploded. A bomb – later discovered in a radio-cassette recorder inside a suitcase in the cargo hold – had ripped a hole in the fuselage, and the plane dived straight to Earth from 31,000 feet. Until the dreadful events of September 11th 2001, it was one of the largest acts of international terrorism investigated by the FBI, and it remains the deadliest terror attack in UK history. As large sections of the plane crashed haphazardly across residential streets in the town of Lockerbie, the bomb also claimed the lives of 11 residents. Debris was scattered over a radius of 845 square miles, and the FBI – working with Scottish authorities – later uncovered 319 tonnes of wreckage.

It was an unprecedented, almost otherworldly thing to have befallen the people of Scotland. The media spotlight had abated little since that terrible day, and each anniversary brought fresh pain. By 1990, the country was still reeling. But there were signs that people were beginning to look ahead, starting to rally, even to celebrate again.

On 14th July, over 30,000 Scots gathered in the city of Stirling to celebrate "A Day for Scotland" in the shadow of Stirling Castle. It was an outdoor, family-friendly festival, an all-day fete designed to showcase the best of Scotland's music, theatre, comedy and politics. The country was ruled from Westminster back then, but not for long; by 1999, Scotland achieved its devolution and Holyrood was established as the site of the Scottish Parliament.

Stirling lies just an hour north west of Stow. The sleepy lanes and quiet rustling of animals contrasted with the pomp and music, the dancing and parties. But it was likely that even the most remote of places would have experienced an increase in traffic on 14th July – Scots and non-Scots alike travelled from all over to attend the festival, perhaps stopping on the way to visit relatives or hire a summer cottage for a few days. It was busier than usual.

In Stow, a 53-year-old retired postmaster named David Herkes was busy mowing his front lawn. The whirr of the lawnmower buzzed intermittently, sending bright tufts of damp grass into the air before they settled. He rubbed his brow, glancing up at the white clouds as they drifted above. The air was still, settled. He'd carry on for another half hour, then head indoors for a cold drink.

Across the street, he noticed a white van parked on the edge of the pavement. A scruffy-looking man was standing by the windshield, wiping it down by hand. David didn't recognise the man or the van, but noted his unkempt appearance. He wondered, dimly, what the bloke was up to. Perhaps he was a friend of a neighbour; perhaps his van just needed a quick clean. The roads here were dusty, especially off-country, and he may well have been out hiking or camping for all David knew. He didn't register too much else, and bent his head once more to the garden.

The sun beat down as he turned to see Ella Mackey,[21] his six-year-old neighbour and the daughter of a local police officer, come rushing down the street. Her shoes – clean, black lace-ups – slapped the pavement as she jogged by, grinning. David waved, smiled and carried on with what he was doing. It was nice to see the kids out enjoying the weather: still nicer that they could, here in Stow. It was a relaxed, gentle sort of place – by and large children could roam free.

David finished the next strip of lawn and turned, back to where the van still stood.

For a moment he stared and then frowned. His head turned slowly to one side as he took in what he was witnessing.

Underneath the open passenger door of the van, David could see Ella's shoes – the same sensible black ones that had just tripped with such energy down the street. Beside them were those of a man. In what seemed like the blink of an eye, the little girl's feet vanished, the man's feet followed, the car door slammed and the van's ignition roared into life. The postmaster switched off the lawnmower, opening his mouth to yell out as the vehicle took off at speed.

David Herkes was willing to give almost anyone the benefit of the doubt: especially in a small, tight-knit community like theirs. People knew one another, they helped each other, they waved and smiled – just like he and Ella had done. But David had never seen that white van before. For a moment he stood, paralysed, wondering if he was over-reacting. Perhaps Ella knew the man – after all, he'd not heard a scream, nor witnessed any sort of struggle.

He stared as the van turned sharply into the right-hand lane and the engine roared. Without fully realising what he was doing, he decided. The speed of it all didn't feel right – the way the child was there one moment and gone the next, the velocity of the van as it took off down the street. Grabbing a pen from his shirt pocket, David peered as he jotted down the licence-plate number, before running inside to call the police.

Minutes later, the sweat pouring down his face, he dashed headlong down the road. The lurch from a peaceful, standard Saturday to this, whatever this was, was absolute. He reached the Mackeys' house and hammered on the door. It was opened after an agonising few seconds' wait.

"She's gone," said David, breathless, his hands on his knees. "Ella."

It was Ella's father's day off. Constable Mackey was dressed in casual clothes: slacks and a loose-fitting shirt. The weekend newspaper was folded neatly in his hand.

"Gone? Gone where?"

"In a van," David panted. "He took her. Just drove off that way." He pointed ahead, where the A7 wound its way north west all the way to Edinburgh. Constable Mackey felt his hand clench the paper, an involuntary movement, swift and reflexive. He stared at David, attempting to make sense of it. Then – with the training of a policeman used to acting quickly, and without emotion – he nodded once, called out to his wife and hurriedly pulled on his boots.

"I've got the number plate," said David. "I wrote it down."

"And you told them, when you rang?"

"Yes."

"Good man. What colour was the car?"

"It was a van. White. Scruffy-looking bloke."

There was little information to go on. Precious minutes had passed. The notion that Ella might, at this very moment, be transported away from Stow and on to God knew where was horrific, unthinkable.

Constable Mackey had seen her not 15 minutes before. For a moment he wondered whether David might be losing his mind, mistaken somehow, whether he'd even seen Ella at all. But something in the other man's eyes, some terrible panic, raised his hackles. David and Mackey ran onto the main road, in the direction of the open fields outside the main village.

The police arrived, tyres screeching – an unfamiliar sound here. One stood before David, notepad flipped open to a fresh page, scribbling down the words as the ex-postmaster described what had happened. Friends and neighbours were starting to emerge from their own houses now, alerted by the sirens and the flashing lights. Not an hour before, the air had been still save for the sound of David's lawnmower; now, hands flew to mouths and brows were furrowed.

Volunteers jumped behind the steering wheels of their own cars and set off down the lane, armed with the van's plate, make and colour, and a vague description of the man they sought. More police cars arrived, jostling for space on the pavements.

Constable Mackey gazed around at the worried faces, the stricken expression on his wife's face, the pacing of the officers as they collected the information. He knew his presence in the midst of the operation would likely do more harm than good at this stage – and besides, he wasn't fit for much at present. Possibilities crowded his mind, turning over one another like a viper's nest. It was all he could do not to press his fingers into his eyes, blocking out the thoughts as they threatened to overwhelm him. Here was a parent who knew every grim statistic about missing children, who'd been trained to speak with bereaved families, stony-faced fathers and weeping mothers. He knew what they were up against, and their main adversary, as every bleak second passed, was time.

"How're you doing?" asked a gruff voice behind him. It was his sergeant, a quick but no-nonsense man who moved with uncommon speed for a burly grandfather fast approaching retirement; Mackey had always liked him.

"I'm fine," the younger man responded. "Just want her found."

"We'll get her back, lad. Go and be with your wife. She doesn't look well."

He was right. Mrs Mackey was leaning on two of their neighbours. One had already run inside her own house to fetch a tumbler of brandy. Her eyes snapped up as her husband approached. "What did he say?" she cried, looking toward the sergeant.

"Just that they're doing all they can. We'll have her back in no time."

As he spoke the words, Constable Mackey dreaded the alternative: the one he knew, in his bones, they were heading inexorably towards. Ella was gone. She had been gone now for minutes, and in minutes a great deal of dust can cover a set of tracks. His colleagues were walking the street, attempting to make out tyre prints. Nothing, it seemed, had been left behind when the van made off with Ella. If it wasn't for David, they'd never even have known she was gone.

In the distance, there came the faint but unmistakable rumble of an engine. The patrol cars had either found something, then, or some poor bugger was about to find themselves having to reverse – this street was now a crime scene. They would never be able to get around the police cars.

Ella's father strained his ears as the sound drew closer. It was hard to tell exactly where the car was – the trees had a habit of obfuscating sound, of confusing noise. It was either some distance away still or right there, about to turn the corner and approach the little village of Stow.

David Herkes heard it too. The low, guttural rumble of the engine, though, sounded different to the cars that had arrived moments before, their lights flashing, their motors still idling. With nothing left to do now he'd told the police everything he could, he stood for a moment and listened, attempting to zone out the other noises vying for attention.

No, this was no ordinary car engine. It reminded him of the vehicle he'd used all those years while delivering the post. It was the noise of a van.

As the first glimpse of a white bonnet flashed into view, the crowd as one seemed caught in slow motion. The sergeant held his pen aloft over his notepad. A woman gasped. The van continued along the road, appearing suddenly to slow. The villagers of Stow could tell that the driver – whoever he was – had not expected to find the little place so busy. The van paused momentarily before accelerating wildly towards them.

"That's him!" shouted David, pointing. It was as though someone else was speaking, someone else shouting the words. His eyes were wild. Every hair on his arms stood on end. "That's the van!"

Almost immediately a police officer – the one who'd taken David's statement – stepped out in front of it, forcing the driver to swerve onto the side of the road. It clipped the pavement, lurching like a drunk as it bumped a hedgerow. The engine was cut. The van was still.

The people of Stow – even those who weren't there – would remember this moment for many years. From shock to horror before swinging haphazardly to awe, emotions veered from one level of intensity to another. Here was Ella's father dashing toward the passenger door, wrenching it open, paying no attention to the man sitting shocked in the driver's seat. He glanced around, threw it shut and raced to the back doors.

One brief lift of the hinge and they were open, swinging wildly back on themselves. He dived inside, emerging seconds later with a limp-looking sleeping bag. Laying it on the ground, he unzipped the top to see a pair of small feet, no shoes or socks. He pulled the bag open and found his daughter, almost suffocated. Her eyes were glazed and confused, but she was breathing. A moment of intense stillness washed over her father as he stared at her. The silence before a wave breaks, before the crash of surf on the shore. He cradled her in his arms, moving backwards to allow officers to rush forward. And then, with a deafening crash, noise returned.

He stood watching as the police moved to pull the driver from his seat. He was unresisting, co-operative even. They bent him over the hood of the van to cuff his hands behind his back. Constable Mackey watched it all, his fists clenched. And then he strode over.

"That," he spat, "is my daughter. "What have you done to her, you bastard?"

The man turned his eyes on Mackey and the world fell away. A startling, piercing blue, they were like stones forgotten at the bottom of the ocean, brushed by waves which made no impression. They were deep, fathomless. Empty. As he was led away by police keen to remove the culprit from Constable Mackey's reach, the man said nothing. Just stared at the villagers, back at the van, at the sky as the clouds turned from dazzling white to grey.

Constable Mackey stared after him. There was something, definitely something...

The set of the jaw, perhaps, or the shape of his face. Even as he watched him being marched quickly to a waiting police car, even as he dipped his head into the passenger side, even as the door clicked smartly shut and he heard the PCs arranging to meet back at the station, Constable Mackey knew he couldn't kid himself. It was the eyes he recognised. He had seen them before. Those were eyes that lingered in the mind. Something unsettling about them, almost feral, inhuman. They burned through you.

He was scruffy, just as David had described, with a mop of untidy dark hair. His clothes looked unwashed, his shoes scuffed. He wasn't tall, around five foot seven. A strange, silent figure with expressionless eyes. Mackey could hear his wife sobbing as the medics helped Ella into another car, and knew there would be time for this later. For now, he needed to be with his child – they were going to the hospital, and fast.

"Who is he?" David asked, appearing at the constable's elbow. "Did you get a name?"

"Nothing yet," said Constable Mackey grimly. "We'll get there though."

The man was driven south for questioning, a half hour journey of 14 miles, to Selkirk Police Station. The officers sat in front, tense and uneasy. What they had just witnessed seemed incredible. The call had come in, frantic and panicked, and the officers had responded. In all likelihood, they may have wondered whether the caller wasn't over-reacting a little. Perhaps the girl had asked for a lift, or a family friend had taken her for a quick spin. Just because the retired postmaster didn't recognise the guy, didn't mean the girl had left with a stranger. Nobody really felt that they were dealing with an abduction until the van roared back into sight, until the back doors revealed the pitiful outline of the poor kid in the sleeping bag. And now they had the guy, and he was chattering away like they'd arranged to meet for coffee.

"Should have been yesterday you pulled me in," he was saying now.

"How's that?" said the officer driving the car. His colleague noticed how tightly set his jaw had become. There was something unsettling about the bloke. In the rear-view mirror, he could see him smiling. His teeth were broken and yellow – like a cartoon villain, like a caricature.

"Well, Friday 13th and all."

There was a pause.

"Unlucky day. And there was that crash up in Edinburgh, eh. That happened yesterday. And now today I land myself with you two. So, it should have happened yesterday. Really unlucky."

He sounded relaxed, calm even. Unmistakably Scottish, too. It was either a front, this blasé, relaxed attitude – or they were dealing with something even more dangerous than could be supposed. Perhaps the man really didn't have any interest in trying to defend what he'd done.

At the police station, he freely admitted to having abducted the child in Stow. It was, he said, "a rush of blood to the head", an impulsive decision he now regretted and would like treatment for. It appeared he knew there was little point in denying his actions – there was no room for manoeuvre. And what was more, his victim could talk.

What the man had done that day was undoubtedly serious, but the police had intercepted him, he'd admitted to his crimes and they could charge him. He was led to a cell while officers completed the necessary paperwork.

At the hospital, Mackey sat with his head in his hands. His wife was in the consulting room with Ella. She'd barely said a word since they'd pulled her from the van.

Oh God, the van. They'd searched it, of course. A dirty old mattress, a Polaroid camera, various ropes and items of children's clothing. The whole thing should be set on fire, but they needed it – every last item was removed, bagged up and labelled.

He shook his head, trying to clear it. He ran his hands through his hair. The fact they were here, right now, as a family, seemed incredible. Impossible. He realised with a jolt that Ella had been missing for half an hour, but he had known – had felt in his bones – that he would never see her again. He had given her up as gone, vanished, disappeared. Without even consciously understanding it, his brain had leapt forward across minutes, days, weeks. The newspaper report next morning, a follow-up the day after and then… nothing.

Who was interested in a little village like Stow? Ella would be forgotten as quickly as she'd been snatched. He'd already seen, as in a premonition, himself and his wife attempting somehow to rebuild their lives. Perhaps confirmation of their worst fears would arrive, perhaps it would not. He'd heard the stories – so many of them – about teenagers who left and never came home. At least their parents could be assured they'd left of their own free will. It seemed hideous to have been conjuring up a future without his six-year-old.

But why shouldn't he? What had happened today was unprecedented, he knew that. Abductions never ended like this, rare as they were. The perp panicked, realised he could be incriminated. The child became a liability. Suddenly abduction transformed, ugly and sharp-toothed, to murder. Most families whose kids were snatched didn't sit in waiting rooms, as he did now, waiting for their child to explain what had happened in that missing 30-minute window. Most families never got any explanation at all.

Mackey sat up, staring straight ahead and frowning. Something had surfaced. A dim memory now, faded with time. He remembered being impressed at everything, back then – all the tricks and techniques used by the police to help witnesses recall what they'd seen, heard, felt. The sniffer dogs and their incredible ability to detect that microscopic particle of scent, the way they chased it, noses to the ground. The brushes and gentle strokes of finger-print collection at a crime scene. He distinctly recalled wondering – and wonder was the right word – how, with a few well-timed questions, prompts and queries, sketch artists had built up portraits as recognisable as photographs.

One of the first times he'd seen that technique used was when the Portobello kid went missing. Those parents in Scotland, the family who lived close to the sea. She'd been out on the promenade and vanished. Good few years ago, seven maybe, or eight… He closed his eyes, remembering. He was a rookie at the time, freshly inducted to the ranks of the police, keen to get his feet under the table. What was her name? The wee blonde lass. Those poor parents, he remembered thinking, empathising without fully looking the horror in the face.

Mackey froze, his eyes fixed wide and staring. Portobello. The girl was in a party dress. She was found days later – a couple of weeks at most. They'd had to identify her through a locket she wore, the bands in her hair. Unrecognisable after God knew how many days dumped like so much rubbish on a roadside. She was miles and miles from where she'd been taken.

A witness had sat down with the sketch artist and all the forces in Scotland had been sent a copy. Every week the *Police Gazette* would arrive and every week all members of the force were expected to read it before their shift. It contained information, appeals and sketches relating to nationwide crimes. It was easy enough to forget once the day began; the calls came in and, soon enough, the next gazette would arrive. But that is how Mackey came across the picture, the drawing of a suspect. He'd studied it carefully, they all had.

He stood up suddenly, his legs shaking. He wasn't sure if it was adrenaline, fear or exhaustion propelling his mind forward, forging connections that didn't exist – but his instincts were usually good ones.

That sketch, all those years ago... He wasn't grasping at straws, he knew that. The man he'd seen on the street that day, the man who'd bundled his child into a van and torn away... it was the same person.

Part Four

"Tremendous. Well done boys"

BLACK

That summer's day in Stow marked the end of one part of the story. But to really understand how a terrified six-year-old was found in a van in rural Scotland, or how a child delivering newspapers, visiting family or just out for a walk collided with those events in 1990, we need to look back – to the beginning.

It was highly unlikely, police knew, that the man who'd attempted to abduct Ella Mackey was a first-time offender. To kidnap a person, especially a child, in broad daylight so close to home revealed a level of confidence, of cunning, of arrogance. This would not be his first crime. Whoever it was, his capture could not have come soon enough.

Serial killers – and particularly those who commit crimes against the most vulnerable members of society – do not emerge fully fledged. There are common themes to their upbringing, to their lives before they enter these darkest of rooms.

A fully functioning society should be equipped to spot early signs of danger; while every offender is different, there are enough similarities to suggest some common red flags. As a child they may be quick to anger, lonely, destructive, they may hurt animals, wet the bed, set fires. As an adolescent, things escalate to intense fantasies fuelled by isolation, bullying, abuse and a sense of inferiority that becomes deeply internalised. Over time, these injustices coalesce, like limescale in a kettle. They form a hard crust. At any time, a person or event may change the course of a life, alter the road from one of death and despair to one of help, therapy, a sense of reconstruction. But if no such help appears, the wounds continue to fester.

The man arrested in Stow was an outlier from the start. He was born in 1947, as the after-effects of the Second World War were slowly starting to recede, leaving a changed society in their wake. After six long years, no one could quite believe it was over at last. It was impossible to remember a time without constant fear, fighting, battles won or lost, telegrams which shattered lives. Nobody was spared from the disruption, chaos and heartbreak brought about between 1939 and 1945, and indeed in the years before that, as rumours bubbled away below the surface. Now, it seemed, countries were expected to simply get on with things again.

The British Empire – once so far-reaching and powerful – was crumbling as colonies broke away and declared independence. Britain's place on the global map was slowly diminishing and there was little energy to prevent it. At home the Beveridge Report had, in 1942, outlined a brave new world of reform, a road map for social-policy change in post-war Britain. Instead of the so-called "five giants" – idleness, ignorance, disease, squalor and want – British society would involve a "cradle to the grave" system of publicly financed measures designed to tackle the inequalities that held the country back. By 1947, that report's key tenet was about to be launched, with a healthcare system based on delivery of services free of charge and at the point of need. The NHS was born.

On February 10th, the Allies signed a peace treaty with Italy, Hungary, Romania, Bulgaria and Finland. The concept of unified blocs intended to rally against a common enemy was taking particular priority, and with good reason – that year also represented the first in a new challenge that would last some 44 years. The Cold War had begun. For the next four decades, the West would be gripped in an ever-escalating crisis that seemed so at odds with the chaos and visible damage wrought in the early 1940s.

The winter of that year was remarkable, too. The UK experienced its worst snowfall of the 20th century and, as few people owned private cars, the disruption – especially to rail services – was felt acutely. Later, in March, temperatures rose steadily and the River Thames was flooded following those long, frozen months of winter. The ice was thawing.

The devastating winter of 1946–7 was accompanied by a series of air disasters as commercial flights became more popular. The post-war boom in aviation – which had previously been reserved for the rich and famous, or diplomats on business – was in full swing, and the industry was expanding rapidly with the aim of carrying far more passengers and freight than was previously considered possible. Newer, faster aircraft and novel prototypes were being launched into the sky. As January 1947 drew to a close, a KLM Douglas DC-3 plane crashed just after take-off in Copenhagen; all 22 passengers on board died, including the second-in-line to the Swedish throne, Prince Gustaf Adolf, and the American opera star Grace Moore.

On April 21st, the young Princess Elizabeth – then on holiday with her parents and sister Margaret, made a radio broadcast from South Africa:

On my twenty-first birthday I welcome the opportunity to speak to all the peoples of the British Commonwealth and Empire, wherever they live, whatever race they come from, and whatever language they speak.

Let me begin by saying thank you to all the thousands of kind people who have sent me messages of good will. This is a happy day for me; but it is also one that brings serious thoughts, thoughts of life looming ahead with all its challenges and with all its opportunity... Although there is none of my father's subjects from the oldest to the youngest whom I do not wish to greet, I am thinking especially today of all the young men and women who were born about the same time as myself and have grown up like me in the terrible and glorious years of the Second World War.

Will you, the youth of the British family of nations, let me speak on my birthday as your representative? Now that we are coming to manhood and womanhood it is surely a great joy to us all to think that we shall be able to take some of the burden off the shoulders of our elders who have fought and worked and suffered to protect our childhood.

We must not be daunted by the anxieties and hardships that the war has left behind for every nation of our Commonwealth. We know that these things are the price we cheerfully undertook to pay for the high honour of standing alone, seven years ago, in defence of the liberty of the world. Let us say with Rupert Brooke: "Now God be thanked who has matched us with this hour"… I declare before you all that my whole life whether it be long or short shall be devoted to your service and the service of our great imperial family to which we all belong.

In Grangemouth, a town 25 miles west of Edinburgh, the River Forth spilled out on its way towards the Scottish capital and off to the North Sea. While the British princess thanked her well-wishers and greeted the world, a woman gave birth. Perhaps the radio broadcast played at the hospital, the midwives carefully listening in.

Grangemouth was established in the 18th century as a link between the Forth & Clyde Canal and the River Forth. It has a proud history of industry, from the petrochemical plants that dot its landscape, to the port, with its busy comings and goings, a container terminal and deep, freezing water. Grain and timber were its chief imports, while coal was exported in vast quantities.

The child's mother, Jesse Hunter Black, lived in a cottage within the gates of the docks. She did not specify his father's name on his birth certificate, and it has never been revealed. Jesse named her child Robert.

The social stigma associated with single motherhood was high; as a result, she planned to have the boy adopted. Robert, too, would be ostracised as an illegitimate child born out of wedlock.

Weeks after his birth, Jesse placed her son in the care of social services and left. She had decided to emigrate to Australia: it is unknown how or with what means, but it's clear she wanted to be as far away as possible from Scotland, from the "shame" of her likely unplanned pregnancy and, as a result, her son. Despite sharing her surname with the child, they never saw one another again, and 50 years after giving birth she died in Australia.

On July 9th, King George VI announced the engagement of his eldest daughter and heir to Lieutenant Philip Mountbatten. The wedding took place at Westminster Abbey that November in an incredible display of pageantry, and was the first of its kind to be televised. The King, who'd recently celebrated his 50th birthday, had just five years to live.

Meanwhile, in Scotland, Robert was about to move to a foster family. Aged six months, in October 1947, he was taken from Grangemouth to the rugged wilderness of the Scottish Highlands. His new guardians were a couple called the Tulips, Jack and Margaret, who lived at Kinlochleven. They were experienced foster carers, both in middle age: Mrs Tulip was well-known for taking on children with a troubled start in life and had fostered many of them over the years.

In June, the Doomsday Clock – a device for measuring the Earth's proximity to a global, man-made disaster – was launched. The clock was maintained by members of the Bulletin of the Atomic Scientists, and remains, to this day, a symbol of the threats faced by humanity, the ultimate catastrophe being represented by midnight. It was set, in 1947, at 11.53, seven minutes to the hour. The world's proximity to apocalypse is assessed in January of each year, and in the 75 years since, it's been moved backward eight times and forward twice as many. Nuclear war and climate change have both played their part. The furthest from midnight was achieved in 1991, and unsurprisingly, the nearest the clock has ever been to midnight is 100 seconds, in both 2020 and 2021.

Kinlochleven is an idyllic, picturesque village situated at the tail end of Loch Leven; trails pass along the banks of the river to Glencoe, rising majestically in the distance. Waterfalls and dense green forest surround the area, with fallen trees covered over in vibrant moss, sprouting toadstools. It's a fairy-tale sort of place, ethereal and quiet. Loch Linnhe snakes all the way into Fort William and the base of Ben Nevis: it's deep, dark and cold.

Situated on the West Highland Way, Kinlochleven is best known for smelting aluminium using hydroelectricity from the nearby mountains. It was once a major local employer and continued to operate until 2000, when it was converted into a power station connected to the National Grid. Kinlochleven was the first village in the world to have every house connected to electricity: the Electric Village, as it came to be known, boasted several impressive buildings attached to the smelting plants. These have now been converted into climbing centres, local breweries, shops and coffee bars. The steep mountains nearby offer long hiking routes and biking trails. Far from the industrial reputation it had held for so long, it's now a major tourist hotspot.

It was common practice in the 1940s and 50s to rehome adopted or fostered children far from their urban birthplaces

– Kinlochleven could not have provided a more beautiful, rugged and outdoorsy starting point, a far cry from the life the boy might have otherwise experienced.

From the beginning, Bobby Tulip – as he was now known – was a troubled child. Once school began, he was teased mercilessly by the other children and had few friends.

When he was five years old, in 1952, Robert's foster father Jack passed away, and he began wetting the bed after a series of terrifying nightmares. For this, he was beaten by his foster mother. When Robert was 11, Margaret Tulip also died. It was unfortunate to say the least, particularly since the couple had – for better or worse – provided the boy with a stable home almost since birth. That said, standards of discipline were incredibly high with the Tulips, so it's hard to tell exactly how much the young Robert Black would have mourned their passing.

Many years later, Black would inform prison psychologists that sex and genitalia had long been a source of fascination. He recalled how from the age of five onwards, several separate incidents occurred revealing a developing interest in girls his own age, and in the physical differences between adult women and children. Black later revealed that, on seeing the genitals of a female neighbour, he developed a belief that he should have been born a girl. At Highland dances from the age of seven, for example, he remembered attempting to look up the skirts of local women and girls.

At the same time, former classmates recalled his desire to subjugate and control younger children, all whilst being bullied by his contemporaries. He was known for his frequent tantrums and the ease with which he vandalised school property. A portrait was emerging of both a victim and perpetrator, someone who picked on those younger than himself while also being bullied.

Though little is known about the exact circumstances of Robert's time with the Tulips, what is certain is Margaret's insistence on personal hygiene. Robert, it seemed, was resistant from a young age. At school, he became known as "Smelly Bobby Tulip" and was mercilessly teased – yet, unusually, did nothing to address the problem. Much later, locals would recall bruises evident on Robert's face, arms and legs. When asked how he'd got them, the boy responded they were the result of fights with his classmates. Jack and Margaret Tulip were strict, no-nonsense sort of people, and in later interviews Black described the beatings that would accompany each incident of bed-wetting at home, of which there were many.

Who knows how badly the Margaret's death affected him. Presumably his feelings were mixed. On the one hand the couple had raised and cared for him in idyllic surroundings for as long as he could remember. On the other, they'd subjected him to what, by modern standards, would be classed as dreadful physical abuse.

Robert was placed with another foster family in Kinlochleven, a short-lived arrangement. By this point Black – he'd changed his surname again – was 11, and it was then that he committed his first known sexual assault, dragging a young girl into a public lavatory. His foster mother, horrified at the incident, reported it to police and rang social services, insisting Robert be relocated.

After over a decade in the quiet, mountainous Highlands, Black was moved to the north east of Glasgow. At a loss, and with few families willing to adopt or rehome an 11-year-old, he was now in the care of Redding Children's Home, a mixed-sex facility near Falkirk.

It didn't take long for this to fall apart. Black frequently exposed himself to other children and was soon sent to another care home for boys in Musselburgh, east of Edinburgh, where he enrolled at Musselburgh Grammar. At school he was reported to be slightly above average academically, with a keen interest in football, table tennis, swimming, athletics and weightlifting. Nonetheless he remained friendless, largely ignored by his peers. It was here, also, that Black was subjected to three years of sexual abuse by a male staff member.

By the age of 15, when Black left, he had experienced his fair share of loss, abandonment, bullying and abuse. Swimming seemed to provide some measure of comfort, and he would often walk to nearby Portobello, which had two pools.

It was now 1963. With the aid of child-welfare agencies, Black moved to another boys' home in Greenock and got a job as a butcher's delivery boy. Despite later confessing to molesting as many as 40 children during this time, the incidents were never reported. He was arrested that same year for luring a child to an air-raid shelter, promising to show her a litter of kittens, before strangling her until she lost consciousness. She was later found wandering the streets, confused and bleeding; she was able to identify the culprit the following day. Despite the sexual nature of the crime, subsequent psychiatric examinationssuggested it was an isolated incident, and that the 15-year-old Black was not in need of rehabilitative treatment.

The following five years saw a string of red flags. Black moved back to his native Grangemouth and lodged with an elderly couple; he molested their nine-year-old granddaughter whenever she came to visit. Although he was evicted, the couple did not inform the police.

After losing his job at a builders' supply company, he moved back to the peaceful shores of Kinlochleven to live with a couple and their six-year-old child. This couple, on discovering Black's crimes against their daughter, did report him to the police.He pleaded guilty to three counts of indecent assault against a child and was sentenced to a year at a borstal in Falkirk, designed specifically to rehabilitate serious young offenders.

Even the word is enough to bring back shudders from those unlucky enough to have been sent to a borstal. Named after a prison in Kent, south-east England, these facilities took in boys mostly between the ages of 16 and 23 in an effort to prevent the chances of their reoffending. The majority of sentences lasted anywhere between two and three years, and the programme involved a strict combination of physical and mental activities, tasks, clubs and courses. Borstal boys undertook eight hours' work a day and received training in cookery, carpentry, bricklaying and farming, for example.

These vocational courses were combined with theatre, music, sports and camping.

Punishments for bad behaviour included being banned from certain privileges, confinement to a room for a period of time and being denied food. Although corporal punishment was explicitly forbidden, hundreds of reports have since emerged detailing the abuse suffered by young men across the UK during the 1970s and 1980s. The Secretary of State for Scotland once raised a question in Parliament relating to Robert Black's borstal near Falkirk, where a particular type of solitary confinement saw boys placed in underground cells for weeks on end. Both physical and sexual abuse – perpetrated by staff and fellow "inmates" alike – seems to have been rife. Tobacco was a precious commodity, often used for bartering or "taxing" against protection money from the "captains" or "daddies", namely the bigger, older or stronger boys.

In 1982, the Criminal Justice Act abolished the system and replaced all borstals with young offenders' units, or youth custody centres. In years to come, Black refused to speak about this time in his life. Borstal was off topic, a segment of time guaranteed to elicit little to no response at all. The only snippet of information that police could glean was simple: whatever had happened in Falkirk, Black had vowed never to find himself imprisoned again.

Are killers born or made? For decades, if not centuries, the question has preoccupied police, criminologists, families of victims torn apart by something they could never have imagined happening. What vital synapse has snapped, what link between brain and body is missing? Psychologists have conducted lengthy, year-long experiments trying to decide exactly this, while neuroscientists have pored over brain scans, hoping to spot the markings of a particular pattern.

Cesare Lombroso, a 19th-century Italian doctor, became one of the country's most celebrated criminologists and believed firmly that individuals were "born criminal". Using a variety of methods, Lombroso suggested that murderers were less evolved than the average citizen, and that physiognomy and "anthropological criminology" – essentially, the way in which a person looks and behaves – could demonstrate recurrent themes and traits in those convicted of violent crime.

In the 1870s, Lombroso worked among such criminals in a Turin prison, slowly building the argument that the shape of a face or the length of an arm could parallel a person's predilection for murder. Crucially, he posited the theory that the brains of violent criminals were fundamentally different to those of non-violent ones.

On the whole, Lombroso's theories have been largely discredited in the modern age. However, since the 1980s, when functional brain scanning has become more prevalent, the idea that the make-up of the brain could have a bearing on violent behaviour was upheld. British neuroscientist Professor Adrian Raine set out to study the brains of convicted murderers in California, and discovered that almost all of them revealed atypical changes, especially with regards to the area which controls emotion, expression of personality, the way we interact and behave socially and how we make decisions.

Brain scans of convicted murderers revealed less activity within these areas. Physical abuse inflicted in childhood – beatings, shakings, blows to the head – are often at least partly to blame for this, since the pre-frontal cortex is especially vulnerable to damage. This in turn creates an inability to control certain emotions and – often as a result of said trauma – a frequent tendency to rage, poor impulse control and various mental-health problems.

The desire to understand what motivates murderers has also extended to genetic study. Advances in neurocriminology – the link between brain function and criminality – have suggested lower levels in offenders of the so-called "warrior" gene (MAOA, or monoamine oxidase A), which is responsible for processing neurotransmitters like dopamine and serotonin – the "reward" and "happy" hormones.

Those with lower levels of the gene demonstrated higher levels of violence and aggression across a range of studies. They were more negatively affected by bad experiences and revealed a comparative lack of emotion when it came to harming other people. In short, they were hypersensitive but also lacking in empathy: a perfect storm.

If low levels of the gene are combined with childhood physical abuse, a person is more likely to commit violent crime. The study concluded that around 30% of men were born with the warrior gene, but it doesn't always reveal itself in outward behaviour. Happily, the majority of children are not subjected to the sort of abuse that triggers it.

As with so much else, there are forks in the road. Moments that could avoid the triggering of violence associated with low levels of the gene, and those that increase their likelihood. That mix of nature – the genes we are born with – and nurture – childhoods free from violence or full of it – seems in negative cases to tip someone into a higher probability of committing violent crime. One can be born with extremely low levels of the MAOA gene and live a happy, comfortable life devoid of violence.

The phrases associated with the most murderous or depraved individuals suggest even the non-scientific public spot the links between genetic make-up and criminality. We might hear suggestions that a killer "had a screw loose", was "mad", or "unhinged". To a large extent these assumptions, however unscientifically phrased, are not entirely false.

There were doubtless opportunities to prevent the evil that Black unleashed. What emerges from his earliest years' offending is the culture of secrecy surrounding abuse: Robert himself was protected by the silence of his victims and their families – keen not to inflict more trauma on their children by dragging them to court – but he'd also kept silence himself. Early beatings from his foster mother Margaret produced visible injuries which were noticed but largely unremarked upon.

The discipline of children and the methods used to obtain it were a different matter in the 1950s, without question, but early interventions may well have seen the child removed from

Margaret's care, encouraged to discuss the death of his foster father, and the fact he himself had been born illegitimate and placed for adoption soon after birth. There was very little, back then, of the more enlightened demand to recognise childhood mental illness and help to treat it early.

When the 21-year-old Black moved to London, he came as an outsider looking for a fresh start. Renting a room at a bedsit near King's Cross station was the first step, but he soon moved – this time to Albion Road, in Stoke Newington. He was to live there for the next three years.

Black's new life in London provided him with a certain amount of anonymity. He was a newcomer in a city of perpetual arrivals and departures, visitors, tourists and businesspeople.

Over the following years, a series of jobs followed – primarily as a lifeguard at various local swimming pools and lidos, and as a barman. There was a brief spell of hope when Enfield Town Football Club invited Black for a trial, but poor eyesight contributed to him not being offered a contract or future opportunities to play with the team.

Locals in pubs around Stoke Newington later recalled him as a loner, an athletic-looking but generally dirty and unwashed regular at darts fixtures – for which, over the years, he won a number of trophies. He drank pints of lager shandies and was often to be found by the fruit machines. There was no overt trouble, but Black never offered information about himself, or struck up friendships with others.

It was in one of these pubs, the Three Crowns, that Black made the acquaintance of a Scottish couple, Edward and

Katherine Rayson, who came from Musselburgh – where Black had been sent to a children's home all those years before. Unusually, Black seems to have discussed his desire to move from Stoke Newington with them, and after developing a friendship of sorts, but primarily out of pity, they invited him to move into their spare attic room in Stamford Hill, a mile and a half north of Albion Road.

For the next 21 years, Black would remain with the Raysons. Much later, in 1994, Eddie Rayson would recall his long-standing lodger as "a perfect tenant. He always paid the rent on time and never gave us any problems." The Raysons were a large family, five sons and two daughters, but no complaint was ever made about Black with regards to the children. Right up until 1990, it was here – in a non-descript, quiet road in suburban London – that he lived. Unobserved, unobtrusive, just going about his life. A strange man perhaps, but not a dangerous one. Nothing to see here.

SUSAN, CAROLINE, AND SARAH

"Can you put me through to Inspector Clark?"

Andrew Watt's palms were sweating profusely. He paced back and forth across the spaces between the officers' desks.

The secretary paused. "He's not in until Monday, I believe. Can I take a message?"

"Get him to call me. It's Andrew Watt. Selkirk Station. Tell him it's urgent."

"Thank you," came the clipped response. "I'll pass it on."

Watt sat beside the telephone, his hands folded together, his heart racing. He glanced up at the clock. They didn't have much time. He wondered what Clark would say. Was he overreacting? Mackey had seemed so sure. And he, Andrew, agreed the likeness was staggering. But he knew it had been a long day. A difficult one. He was tired. Perhaps he was turning a mere hope into reality, making connections where none existed. The man they were holding in the cells was an enigma, a strange, bemused presence who seemed wilfully unaware of the seriousness of his offence. He was either mad or bad or both. Watt knew that Clark, more than anyone else, would want to know. He was right to make that call.

Twenty minutes later the telephone rang, a shrill, insistent interruption to the quiet of the office. Three of Andrew's colleagues sat watching as he lifted the plastic receiver.

"Watt," came the voice down the line.

"Hello Inspector," said Andrew. "I'm sorry to trouble you on the weekend."

"No bother, no bother," said the other man amiably. "What can I do for you?"

"We've arrested a man this afternoon. In Stow."

"Stow?"

"Yes. Completely out of the blue. Suspect grabbed a child from the street and drove off with her. A local guy witnessed it and noted the number plate."

"Good man. How did you get him?"

"Well sir, he came back."

"He what?"

"I know. Very strange. He turned around and headed back through the village. We were there taking statements and not 10 minutes later his van comes back down the road. Kid was in the boot. We got her out. She's fine." Watt closed his eyes on the final two words. Who knew if Ella was fine or not. But she was alive.

"Excellent work." There was a silence. Clark was not one to push his officers or probe when he knew they needed to come to the point themselves.

"So, er, the child's father is one of us, sir. We didn't want him too near the suspect for obvious reasons. But he appears to have recognised him – that's why I called. To let you know."

Again Clark waited.

"PC Mackey – that's the girl's father, sir – well, he thought the suspect looked familiar."

Watt glanced at his fellow officers. He didn't want to waste the gaffer's time. His palms were sweating again. "He thought there was a resemblance between the suspect and the sketch artist's drawing from one of your cases, sir. I'm sorry. The man's very upset, he's in shock, he could be wrong, sir –"

"Detective Superintendent," said Clark carefully, "which case are you referring to?"

"Caroline," said Andrew, at last. "Caroline Hogg. Portobello."

Hector Clark was, by all accounts, the sort of man every constabulary in the country would clamour to work with. Even his physical appearance suggested competence: he was solid but not overweight, with a kind smile and neat, pressed suits. His dark eyebrows arched into a broad forehead that became broader with age. He was reassuring, gentle, no-nonsense.

Born in 1934 in Northumberland, Clark impressed from an early age when it came to football and could well have taken this skill to a professional level. He completed his National Service in the early 1950s and was a member of the RAF before joining the Northumberland County Constabulary in 1955. Soon enough he had been accepted into the CID, the unit reserved for the most serious crimes, and rapidly rose through the ranks, eventually becoming head of the division there. His next promotion was the biggest, and would redefine the course of his investigative career.

With over 70 murders overseen and investigated by Clark, he was appointed Assistant Chief Constable. In 1983, a highly unusual – unprecedented, even – decision was made. Clark would head up a team made up of individual county constabularies – a tough task made even more difficult by the fact that the crimes had been committed both in England and over the border in Scotland, where the law was different and investigative techniques varied from the English system. It was commented on that nobody else could have hoped to succeed in linking these disparate forces.

Clark had been appointed senior investigating officer on a joint murder inquiry relating to the deaths of two children. Their abductions and murders had outraged the public, but whoever had killed Susan Maxwell and Caroline Hogg remained at large.

In July 1982, 11-year-old Susan had asked her mother for permission to play tennis with a friend in her hometown of Cornhill-on-Tweed, close to the Anglo-Scottish border. The Maxwells lived in a farmhouse on the English side. This was the first time the girl had asked to go on her own, and though her mother was torn, she agreed.

Susan was 11 now after all, and the two-mile bike ride into Coldstream wouldn't take more than 15 minutes. But her mother didn't want her to cycle, and insisted she walked instead. Susan left the house wearing a yellow top and carrying her tennis racquet. En route she was offered a lift by a local farmer and arrived to play with her friend as agreed. The pair enjoyed themselves, knocking the ball back and forth over the net as the sun continued to beam down. When they'd finished, they agreed to meet again the next day.

Susan's mother decided – given the heat of the day – that she would drive over to the courts to collect her daughter. She put her younger children, Tom and Jacqueline, into the car and drove the short distance, watching along the roads for her daughter on the agreed route home. There was no sign of Susan.

Two weeks passed of fruitless searching by Northumberland Police, as well as friends and neighbours. Susan's father, Fordyce, was instrumental in leading a number of the searches, barely pausing to eat or sleep. Tracker dogs scanned the country lanes, finding nothing; 300 officers combed the area, expanding the search perimeters to some 80 miles.

Witnesses reported having seen a child matching Susan's description during the course of the afternoon, but sightings stopped at 4.30pm, when Susie crossed a bridge over the River Tweed. One witness, a local woman called Norma Richardson, submitted a written statement to the effect that she left home at 4.15pm on the day of Susie's disappearance, and noticed a girl swinging a tennis racquet in her hand: "I didn't see anyone on the Tweed bridge," she said, "but as I passed over it my attention was taken by a young girl walking on the grass verge. She was about nine or ten years old with short brown hair and wearing a lemon top and white shorts."

Susan's tennis racquet, tennis ball and a blue plastic flask she was known to have with her were never found. Several witnesses came forward to state they had noticed a white van in the area near the tennis club; one statement claimed the van had been parked in a field off an A road.

A local girl, 15-year-old Karen Young, was with her grandparents on 30th July and was one of those who spotted the girl. "I remarked to my grandparents that it was Susie Maxwell," she said. "I knew her and her family and thought it was very unusual for her to be walking alone."[22] Another witness, psychiatric nurse Mark Ball, came forward to report he had seen a child matching Susie's description "hitting out" at a maroon car on the afternoon of her disappearance.

Christine's mother experienced that same creeping dread that April's parents had known, all those years ago, as the world seemed to spin on its axis: the same terrible loss felt by Ann, Mary Boyle's sister, as she became accustomed to life without her twin. And the same bewilderment, fury, confusion of Genette Tate's parents – the void left in their lives and the lack of closure.

For Susie Maxwell's parents, closure of a sort did appear. On Friday 13th August, they took part in BBC Radio's Jimmy Young show. This was exactly the sort of media exposure Liz Maxwell wanted: the show had many millions of listeners up and down the country. Susie's mother drove to the broadcaster's nearest studio at Alnwick Castle, a beautiful 11th-century estate owned by the Duke of Northumberland and dubbed "the Windsor of the North". The setting was at odds with Liz's reasons for visiting, but the drive navigated through some of the north east's most picturesque stretches of coastline. The show was vital to keeping Susie and her story in the public eye.

While Liz described their daughter as a "cautious and sensible girl", police in Staffordshire received a phone call from a member of the public.

"If someone chatted," said Liz on the radio, "she would chat back." There was the possibility that "she thought she knew the person she got into the car with". Clearly there was no doubt in her mind that her child had been taken from the bridge crossing the River Tweed and transported elsewhere. Had Susie's natural gregariousness and outgoing nature proved her downfall?

Immediately after this radio broadcast, Liz returned home. It had been a long and difficult day, but she'd kept her resolve, and asked members of the public to contact police with any relevant information.

As she pulled the car back into the drive of Cramond Hill, she noticed a small group of policemen standing by the front door. Besides the constables the couple had come to expect, Detective Chief Inspector Fred Stephenson was also present. She cut the ignition and stepped out of the car.

Inside the house all was still. Jackie and Tom were at their cousin's house. Fordyce and Liz sat down, as asked, and waited.

"We have found a little girl," said one of the officers. "I've had the police at Uttoxeter on the phone." Mrs Maxwell later described how he struggled to describe the discovery. It seemed to take every ounce of effort to clarify the statement he'd just made.

"This little girl is not alive."

The day before, a lorry driver had made the grim discovery some 250 miles away, in a Midlands layby near the market town of Uttoxeter in Staffordshire. Arthur Meadows, the driver, was initially suspected of murder, and was brought in for questioning by police. Many years later this traumatic event would be recounted by the driver's son, then just 10 years old. Shane Meadows is the director best known for his cult film *This Is England*, and recounts in subsequent interviews the horror of the media being camped outside the family home until it was established that Arty Meadows had simply been in the wrong place at the wrong time.

"We will need the name of Susie's dentist," said one of the officers, as the news settled on the Maxwells like the heaviest blanket. Liz recalled wondering why on earth they'd need this information – back then identity via dental records was far less widespread when it came to unrecognisable human remains. Liz provided officers with a baby tooth of Susan's in addition to the name of her dental practice. Later that afternoon officers returned with confirmation that the body discovered was indeed that of Susie Maxwell.

"Can I see her?" asked Liz.

The officers shifted uncomfortably. What they knew and what they needed to convey to the Maxwells were two very different things.

"It's been very warm," said one of the men, gently.

"I think I really knew what they meant," Liz said later, "and that they were just trying to shield me from the worst of it, but I thought if I had just been able to see her one more time it would have helped. It probably wouldn't have done though. That has struck me a lot, the fact that she was lying outside vulnerable to birds and insects and mice."

Susie's body was in an advanced state of decomposition. The inquest into the cause of death – which took place a full year later – reached an inconclusive verdict.

Unlike the cases of April, Christine, Mary and Ginny, Susie's abduction could be conclusively proved to have ended, devastatingly, in murder. The Maxwells had clear and irrefutable proof that their child was gone. For two weeks, Mrs Maxwell had refused to draw the curtains at home in case her daughter should find her way home. After that fortnight of waiting, her hope was extinguished. They didn't have answers, but the police did have a body.

Susan Maxwell's disappearance had ended in tragedy: the culmination of weeks of media coverage and desperate searching. The body, however, is any victim's final communication to those hell-bent on bringing their murderer to justice. It will speak for the person who can no longer speak for themselves.

Forensic examination of a body and the surrounding crime scene is a well-honed craft. one that develops year on year as technology advances. Investigators knew that the way in which it was handled, transported and stored could all impact the forensic material or evaluation of evidence, potentially allowing the killer to walk free. Clothing and property, or evidence of any kind, must remain in place until photographers have been able to document its appearance and position, and crime-scene investigators have assessed its potential to be moved in such a way as not to lose evidence, which can be destroyed all too easily.

Entomologists examine insects' life cycles to establish not only a time of death, but the relationship between the location of a body when discovered, and where it might have been beforehand. A fortnight had passed since Susie was abducted and despite the inquest's inconclusive results, it appeared likely she had died within 24 hours of being abducted. The Home Office pathologist, Dr Scholz van der Merwe, described her body as "unrecognisable" upon his arrival at a copse near the lay-by where she'd been discovered; and her clothing was the first indicator of her identity.

"I prefer to think that it was all over very quickly," Susie's father Fordyce commented years later, "that she blacked out and didn't really know what was happening. Whether that's true or not I just don't know, but it helps me get through the rest of my life."

For a year, the investigation into Susie's death ploughed onwards. Police filed over half a million hand-written index cards; hours became days became weeks. The officers continued, doggedly pursuing every lead, interviewing hotel staff and travelling communities alike, gathering statements, interviewing and re-interviewing witnesses.

Meanwhile, the Maxwells began to pick up the pieces of their shattered lives. Although the couple continued to receive hundreds of letters – from other parents in similar situations, or whose children had otherwise died young – members of their local community seemed reticent to say Susie's name or discuss the case at all. This habit of obscuring the unthinkable translated to the Maxwells' then five-year-old daughter Jackie, who refused to say her sister's name aloud for many years.

Liz and Fordyce later reported a discussion between themselves and Tom, Susie's brother, who was three at the time of her disappearance. They talked about the future and about what Tom would be like when he was older.

"Will I ever be 11?" he asked, stunning them into silence.

Their son, who'd been so young at the time of Susie's murder, had taken his sister's death as an indicator. Did anyone live past the age she'd been? Like everything else in that dreadful episode, it was deeply disturbing. The ripples of the crime extended into the minds of other victims, those learning about the world in the direst of circumstances, growing up too fast. And of course, the Maxwells couldn't give Tom a certain, cast-iron affirmation – they couldn't convince him beyond doubt that he'd grow up, even if his sister had not. If Susie would remain 11 forever, it seemed natural enough that her brother expected the same.

The seasons changed and a new year began. In February 1983, a 37-year-old civil servant was one of several tenants who hired a plumber to attend their block of flats in north London. Seven months after Susie's disappearance, dismembered human remains were discovered in the blocked drain, and the investigation into the serial killer Dennis Nilsen began.

Octopussy and *The Return of the Jedi* were that year's highest-grossing and most popular films. The Conservatives retained power following the election of 9 June, and Margaret Thatcher was to remain in post. Soon her Chancellor would announce cuts to public spending of some £500million. In July, the country was plunged into a heatwave.

Five-year-old Caroline Hogg had begged her mother to allow her just a few minutes' more playtime. It was Friday 8th July, and the area was enjoying its second major hot-weather spell in as many years. Caroline had spent the afternoon with her mother and grandmother at a friend's party in their hometown of Portobello, a coastal suburb of Edinburgh. Ordinarily the summer months saw an influx of tourists headed for the beach and a few days of sun, but it was a close community and people looked out for one another – and for one another's children. From Caroline's front door, you could see the promenade, and, behind it, the chilly waters of the North Sea. The school term was over; Caroline had just completed her first year at Towerbank Primary. She was the baby of the family, the youngest of five children.

Once they'd dropped her grandmother at the bus stop, Caroline was permitted to travel the short distance down the road to the local playground. This was a journey she'd made many times before. The only stipulation from her mother, Annette, was that she steer clear of strangers and be sure not to cross over into Fun City, the permanent fairground by the harbour. There were clear limits that Caroline knew well. The promenade might have been visible from the front gate, but it was strictly out of bounds without an adult.

Caroline left at around 7pm after swapping her smart shoes for a pair of pink-and-white trainers, at her parents' insistence. She wore a white-and-lilac gingham dress and would have been striking compared to the casual clothes worn by her friends, several of whom spotted her as she made her way into the playground and, later, along the promenade. A photograph taken just hours before her disappearance shows her blonde hair swept back into bunches held by lilac bobbles. She stands still, her eyes curious, looking at something to the left just out of shot. It appears as though she's about to smile – a shy expression, perhaps, or one of concentration. Maybe the children were playing musical statues, which would explain the static nature of her stance. One click of the camera and the music starts again – the kids race off to wait for the next interruption.

Portobello is a bustling seaside town, particularly during the summer and especially on a Friday. Many Scottish families made and continue to make the trip to these coastal stretches, enjoying the beaches, or a pint in the bars that pepper the promenade.

Just 15 minutes later, Mrs Hogg asked her son Stuart to check on Caroline. He returned, breathless, to say that she wasn't at the playground.

For 45 minutes they searched. A local teenager working at the Fun City amusement park came forward quickly to state he had seen Caroline. She rode the roundabout on a little toy bus; her 15p fare had been paid for by a man the boy didn't recognise.

John Hogg, Caroline's father, immediately assumed "she had been enticed away by someone who had been able to gain her trust", adding that "in normal circumstances she would not have gone away with someone she did not know."

Witness statements – mostly from children – confirmed this most chilling assumption. They recounted how a "scruffy" man had been hanging around the playground, watching them all. He smoked a cigarette by a lamppost, one said: "He looked weird." He had moved off, away from the swings, in the direction of the promenade, said another. He seemed drunk. "He needed a shave." But he only moved when he noticed a child in a party dress. Instead of heading home, the girl made her way to Fun City.

She was later seen riding the merry-go-round, something which cost money Caroline didn't have with her. It was therefore assumed the man had paid for the child; he stood waiting for her to climb down and then led her away by the hand. No more sightings of the girl were reported, and given the vast numbers of people who had witnessed her movements prior to this moment, it was assumed she had been taken away by car – indeed Fun City had a car park directly behind it.

On Monday 11th July John and Annette Hogg spoke to reporters in what was to be their only press conference. "We came here today," said John, "hoping if someone sees this at home… just bring her back. If anyone knows anything at all, let the police know. Please, let her come home."

After 10 days, Caroline's body was found in a ditch in Leicestershire, 300 miles away from where she had last been seen, dumped in a lay-by between the little villages of Twycross and Sibson. Pathologists were unable to confirm a cause of death: in fact, when she was discovered by a horrified salesman who'd paused briefly to review some work, it was impossible to tell the age or sex of the child. The hot weather had badly decomposed the remains.

Leicestershire CID began the task of contacting other forces with open missing-children files. When Lothian and Borders detectives were called and given a description, their hearts sank. Their colleagues described a locket found on the body and the lilac hair bands: tiny fragments belonging to the person who would never wear them again, never tie her own hair back or swap out one picture for another in a much-treasured necklace. The items had outlived their owner.

Whatever had happened to both Susan and Caroline, they were both abducted in seemingly random, opportunistic fashion. Whoever had taken them had likely been travelling by car; alarms were raised quickly in both cases, once the children were found to be missing: not enough time to escape on foot, plus no witnesses came forward to report sightings of the children on trains, buses or other public transport. In both cases, the girls had been taken in or near Scotland and murdered at some stage between the crime-scene location and the site of deposition. Caroline's body was discovered south-east of Uttoxeter, where Susan Maxwell had been found a year before – just 30 miles separated them. In both cases, various details – Susan was discovered without her shoes or underwear on, and Caroline was naked – pointed to the motive being a sexual one.

In the space of a single year, then, police across four different forces had now become involved: Northumberland, the site of Susan's abduction; Staffordshire, where she was discovered; Edinburgh, Caroline's hometown; and Leicestershire, where she was found. The Chief Constables of the northern constabularies rarely worked with those of the Midlands, but here they were, joined in this most tragic of operations.

Local newspaper the *Hinkley Times* reported on the grisly discovery of Caroline's body on 22nd July 1983. It described the man police were keen to interview as between 30 and 40 years old and between five foot eight and five foot ten in height. He was of a medium to well-built frame, had collar-length dark wavy hair, wore heavy-framed glasses with tinted lenses, a dark jacket, jeans or cords and brown shoes. It was an astonishing amount of information but the man, despite all these markers, was unobtrusive in appearance, barely noticeable but for being a stranger in Portobello. He was average height, average weight, averagely dressed apart from a certain dishevelled appearance.

"As we went to press," the reporter writes, "the name of the Assistant Chief Constable to lead the hunt was due to be announced."

By the end of the month, Deputy Chief Constable Clark – Hector – was placed in charge.

*

"Rough business."

They were in the Chief's office. The sun was setting on another long day.

Clark nodded. "Yes, sir." It was a week since the discovery of Caroline Hogg's body.

The Chief puffed contemplatively on his cigar. The smoke curled and danced its way across the room. Clark shifted in his seat. If he hadn't been so exhausted, a meeting like this would have made him alert, ready to go, excited even. Instead, he watched the grey eddies as they shifted and settled into the air.

"I want it sorted quickly, Hector," said the Chief. "I've total faith in you." He gave Clark a long look. "Do whatever you have to. People are bloody furious. The press are all over us."

Clark nodded.

"In some ways it's well they might be. We threw everything we had at Maxwell. Nothing. And now this."

Again Clark nodded, then cleared his throat. "To have it happen again like this… in exactly the same way. I think it's one man." The Chief looked at him. "Just one man. Too many similarities."

"I agree the MO fits in both cases. But they could be isolated incidents. It's a fine balance, Hector. Look at them together by all means. But don't try to fit a square peg into a round hole. If something comes up pertaining to Susan Maxwell, you can't try to make it work for Caroline's case too. I don't need to tell you that, but…"

"I know, sir. We'll link them for now. But any evidence to the contrary and we split the forces – Northumbria and Staffordshire, Edinburgh and Leicestershire."

The Chief nodded. His brow cleared. "Any news on witnesses from the lovers' lane?"

Clark shook his head. "Nothing so far."

The *Hinckley Times* had put out an appeal that morning for what the headline euphemistically called "courting couples" to come forward. The lay-by where Caroline was found was a frequent haunt for locals; the reporter suggested police felt it would "save embarrassment" if potential witnesses approached them directly rather than being traced.

The Chief sighed. "And the calls?"

"Still coming in, sir. Over 200 today. People want to help."

"I know. And thank God they do. But we'll miss something if we carry on like this. The teams are exhausted already. How many follow-ups do we have?"

"Heading for a thousand at present. And that's just calls."

"And the road checks?"

"Ongoing. They've been stationed along the A444. Spoken to about five and a half thousand motorists. All of them too bloody nosy for their own good."

"Jesus Christ," barked the Chief. "And no one's seen a bloody thing? It's not possible, Clark. What is he, invisible? A bloody ice-cream man? A woman?"

"We've sent teams out to some of the other villages nearby." Clark listed the names of communities his officers had searched, houses they'd approached, neighbours they'd questioned. "And anyone with time on their hands has been doing the posters." 25,000 of these had been printed, showing the clothes Caroline was wearing when she was last seen in Portobello.

"For heaven's sake. All this and not a single scrap of useful information."

The Chief sat back, his arms folded. The cigar sent its curls of thinning smoke up and out of the window in a single stream.

"We need it solved, Clark."

Hector was rarely one to bow to pressure. He would do what he could – everything he could – but it was a foolish policeman who promised anything when dealing with a crime of this sort.

"He doesn't want to be found," he said, surprising himself.

"What's that?" said the Chief, clearly lost in thought himself.

"Well, that's what makes it so difficult. I know it sounds obvious, but he doesn't want to be found. If it's one man, that is. I'll allow for the slim possibility that these are two separate incidents, unlinked and random in their similarity." He leaned forward. "If it's the same man, he wants to continue. He wants to find kids, kids on their own, preferably out somewhere alone, and he wants to take them. He does whatever he wants with them. And then he kills them and dumps them miles away. That's what drives him. He's done it twice now – that we know of. He'll do it again, no question about it. This is no game: he's not taunting us or trying to beat us. It's almost like he's confident enough not to care."

The Chief was staring at him. He started to nod, slowly. "He doesn't want to be found," he said softly. "That's the last thing he wants. If he's caught, he has to stop."

"And so far, he's succeeded," said Clark. "He's won. We don't have him. We have no idea who he is. We have no witnesses, no numberplates, no fingerprints, no photographs. So we have to make it harder for him. How can we have a thousand phone calls, 5,000 drivers stopped, all those conversations, all those potential clues just scattered around?" He warmed to his theme. He stood up, pacing the room. "I'll bet you, buried somewhere in those stacks of information, is a clue. Something to get us started. Something that makes it harder for him to remain anonymous. We've tried the traditional way, sir. What about something new? We have the technology: it's right there. We just need to use it."

The Chief nodded. He knew what Clark was referring to. "Fine." He ran his hands through his hair. "Yes, I agree. Let's give it a go." He looked dubious but exasperated, almost helpless. "Why not? No harm in trying."

"I'll give a briefing this afternoon. Get the boys to speak to the other forces. It'll take time, sir, but I think this is the best hope we've got."

As Clark closed the door of the office behind him, he heard the Chief's muttered whisper –

"Damned computers."

And so Hector Clark went to work. It wasn't guaranteed to produce results, but any gamble at this stage might just pay off. Perhaps, with a certain amount of tenacity, the processing machines they had at their disposal could help. He had no idea. But it was worth a try.

The notion of using computers for anything in 1983, let alone something as serious as a murder investigation, was alien to most people. Trust came from good old-fashioned pen and ink, white sheets of paper, corkboards on which to pin photographs, notes, directions of inquiry, memos, statements. Filing cards were there for a reason, were they not? And hadn't they always worked pretty well – documenting the calls as they came in, the leads to follow, the avenues to explore?

Although the process would take months, Clark pressed ahead. He ordered members of the team to begin inputting data into a machine: all of it, every last scrap they had on Susan Maxwell and Caroline Hogg. The two cases, and every detail pertaining to them, could then be compared and sifted through. Perhaps this new technology could point them just a little closer to the elusive needle in the haystack, the clue they'd been missing or just couldn't see.

Just two years later, and the criticisms levied at the Ripper investigation had changed operational guidance. Deputy Chief Inspector Clark was now tasked with attempting to digitise findings from the Maxwell and Hogg murders.

Before long, his superiors called time on the operation. Clark would digitise the records pertaining to Caroline's case, but they would continue to work manually on Susan's. He agreed, and they pressed on: one case being investigated as cases always had been, the other serving as a guinea pig, a trial that would either help them track their man or reinforce their failure.

In the meantime, a sketch artist worked with witnesses who had seen Caroline with her presumed abductor at Fun City on that hot July day. The result revealed a mop of unbrushed, almost shoulder-length dark hair, a sparse beard and goatee and a pair of rimmed spectacles. Clark shuddered as he stared at it, wondering at the anguish of the child's parents. And Edinburgh so close by...

The image was widely circulated among police. When Constable Mackey first saw it, his daughter Ella was just two years old.

There was then what seemed a pause, of sorts: no fresh reports, no children plucked off the streets – or at least none that fitted the established pattern. There are many potential reasons for this: killers may often exhibit a "cooling-down" period between crimes; their circumstances might have changed – jobs, money, relationships, living arrangements. Whatever the reason, murders like Susan and Caroline's, police began to hope, were hideous anomalies committed by a madman. Awful one-offs. Rare. They could focus in the meantime on ensuring the cases didn't run cold. For two years now Susan and Caroline's killer had remained on the loose. Police trundled on, making little real progress.

"Where did he go?" muttered Clark, turning the pages of witness statements. It was March 1986. He was tired. The incident room was silent; everyone had left for the day. The large open-plan office had that strange, empty atmosphere that follows a great flurry of activity. Coffee cups sat half-drunk on desks, pens leaked ink onto pads of blotting paper and a fly buzzed round the dehydrated plant somebody had optimistically placed near the window and then forgotten to water.

It was a question he asked himself almost daily. Where was he? Someone as brazen as the person they were looking for was unlikely to simply stop. No – he'd carry on until they stopped him. But they hadn't heard from him, not for years now. Clark was determined to find him, bring him in, look him in the eye. He wanted answers. He wanted to go back to the families of those children and explain. What sort of person committed this type of crime and then simply vanished? Had he moved abroad? Died? Perhaps he'd simply –

The phone rang. "Clark," he said simply. He heard the exhaustion in his own voice.

"Sir," came the voice on the other end. "It's Nottinghamshire." Clark frowned. He had nothing active in Nottingham, as far as he could remember. No leads, no witnesses. "I've been asked to notify you, sir. A child's body was discovered today in the Trent. Missing from Leeds for several weeks now."

Clark closed his eyes. Nottingham was a good 80 miles from Leeds.

"A girl?" Clark asked.

"Yes, sir. Name's Sarah Harper. 10 years old. She'd gone out to buy bread for her mother."

"Who found her?"

"Member of the public, sir. Dog-walker, I believe. He saw something in the water and used a stick to bring it to the bank. He's pretty shaken up."

"And no one saw anything?"

226

"The shopkeeper saw her. Said she bought the bread as usual along with two packets of crisps. Said a strange bloke came in to browse around the same time, then left when Sarah did. Nothing else."

Clark nodded. "Thanks for letting me know. I'll arrange to come first thing tomorrow."

He stood up from the desk, knocking over a flask of long-cold tea. It was an odd feeling, a mixture of fury and adrenaline, almost excitement. He noticed his hands had clenched into fists. The bastard had done it again – of that he was sure. The shark seemed to have swum out to sea all this time, but now here it was again among innocent swimmers with no idea what was lurking, watching, beneath them.

Sarah Harper disappeared between her home in Morley, Leeds, and the corner shop – a distance of less than a tenth of a mile, only two minutes away. K&M Stores sold everything from biscuits to gin, fizzy drinks, household items and groceries. Sarah knew Morley well. The Harpers' home was just moments away from Peel Street Junior School, where she and her sister Claire walked every day. It was also close to the Salvation Army Citadel, where Sarah played cornet in the band.

It was four days before Easter and the children were on holiday. Jacki Harper, Sarah's mother, had taken the girls and her five-year-old son David shopping before they visited local relatives. They'd had tea together and then, as *Coronation Street* ended, Jacki – who was heavily pregnant at the time – asked Sarah to run to the shop for a loaf of bread.

Sarah put on her anorak, left her brother, sister and mother and collected empty lemonade bottles to deposit at the newsagents.

It was a dark, wet night, the last gasps of winter clinging on. She bought the bread on arrival as well as two packets of crisps. It was five minutes past eight. A man stepped inside, appearing to browse and then left without purchasing anything. As Sarah cut down a short alley to get home, she was snatched off the street.

Almost an hour later – after asking her other daughter, Claire, to go out and look for Sarah – Jacki Harper spoke to the shopkeeper, who confirmed Sarah had left the shop shortly after 8pm. With no sightings of her since, the police were called. It was thick with rain outside: no child would want to stay out in weather like this.

There were some differences between Sarah's murder and those of Susan and Caroline, who'd both been abducted at the height of summer. Susan and Caroline had been found in lay-bys along England–Scotland motorway routes, while Sarah had been discovered in a river. It was decided to keep the two investigations – Susan and Caroline, and Sarah Harper – separate, but to maintain regular contact and remain open to the possibility that they were connected. The two investigations would be distinct, but information was shared when necessary.

The thought worried Hector Clark. There were differences, yes, but also common threads that bound the three tragedies. All three were pre-pubescent girls abducted near to their homes and most likely a car had been involved. They had all been taken south and discarded like so much rubbish in the Midlands. The cases came eventually to be referred to as the Midlands Triangle: when plotted on a map, the grim discoveries were less than 30 miles distant from one another.

But it was the third similarity that worried task forces the most. It was clear all three abductions were sexually motivated. Susan Maxwell's underwear had been removed, Caroline Hogg was found naked and Sarah Harper's post-mortem revealed an extensive and brutal sexual assault had taken place. A timeline of the three cases would suggest that the killer, if indeed the same man was responsible, was becoming more violent.

In April 1986, the three cases were featured together on *Crimewatch*, but no leads of substance were called in. The culprit had escaped into the night, leaving no trace.

In early 1988, Hector Clark's forces made contact with the FBI. This was unusual: seeking help from outside police agencies was encouraged but not always acted upon. The United States' Violent Criminal Apprehension Program had been formed in 1985 with the aim of tracking society's most dangerous criminals. Terry Green was its manager when the UK police asked for their input in the case of the three murdered schoolgirls.

Offender profiling was still very much in its infancy. Many senior FBI detectives felt its increasing popularity relied on not much more than pop psychology, that it distracted from traditional policing techniques and hindered investigations.

Traditionally, crimes and their solution had been the remit of crime-scene investigators.

Forensics were key and following the breadcrumbs was considered to be the gold star of policing. No one had really thought about the idea of following a psychological breadcrumb trail, though. And the same attitude prevailed in the UK until 1986, when Professor David Canter, a psychologist from the University of Surrey, drew up a profile that would help police catch the so-called Railway Rapists John Duffy and David Mulcahy.

During the mid-1970s and in crimes spanning at least a decade, Duffy and Mulcahy carried out a string of assaults and murders around various train stations in London and the south west. Canter was working as an architectural psychologist at the time and had studied the connection between people and buildings. His involvement was the first example of offender profiling in Britain, no mean feat considering the crimes occurred within some distance of each other, and the victims' ages ranged between 14 and 32. Not only that, but police were wary about enlisting the help of a man whose speciality seemed so obscure, so unconnected.

Canter began his unenviable task by examining geography: plotting the crimes on a map to establish where the offender(s) might live. He then attempted to classify personality traits, character and patterns by placing offenders into one of two categories, focusing on how the offender interacted with and dealt with the victim, and judging the amount of dominance used. Canter's profile of John Duffy helped police whittle down their 2,000 suspects to just one of two. His predictions were as follows:

The offender lived in either Kilburn or Cricklewood – Duffy was later revealed to live in Kilburn. The offender would be married but have no children – Duffy was indeed married, and was infertile. He would, Canter suggested, have marriage issues – Duffy was separated when the crimes took place. He would be a loner with few friends – Duffy was found to have two friends, one of whom – David Mulcahy – was his accomplice. Canter posited that Duffy would be physically small and unattractive – he was found to be five foot four, with acne. Incredibly, Canter went further: the offender would be a martial artist or body builder – Duffy was a member of a martial arts club. And most damningly of all, his "need to dominate women" as specified in Canter's report proved to be correct – he had a history of violently attacking his wife and had also insisted on tying her up before sex.

Canter went on to develop more in-depth studies of what he termed investigative psychology. As a result, profiling as a useful tool in the police arsenal increased dramatically from the mid-1980s.

A draft profile of the Midlands Triangle murderer was put together based on the details Hector Clark's team provided. Their suspect, read the FBI report, would be male, single, in his late 30s or 40s. Someone who didn't have many friends or family and lived in rented accommodation. He would be itinerant, unfixed, someone who knew the areas he cruised well – even towns and villages far from his home base.

It was likely, the FBI said, that the man they were looking for possessed a large child-pornography collection. In time, the detectives agreed, it would become apparent that the man they were looking for had killed other children too. It was highly unlikely, they felt, that the murder of Susan Maxwell was the killer's first.

There was something confident and brash about it, something almost adept, something... practised.

Lawrence Byford's report into the investigation on Peter Sutcliffe highlighted the problems caused by constabularies working disparately. With no central command, it was impossible to correlate information, check for patterns or establish timelines. "Certain errors of judgement" during the hunt for Sutcliffe "were very serious indeed and were not prevented or ameliorated by the influence of senior investigating officers from other forces."

More than once, Byford said, West Yorkshire Police could have benefited from "independent professional advice", and more than once "chose not to do so". He claimed that forces were suffering from "parochial superiority" that "must be overcome". "I am firmly of the view" he said, "that in the series serious crimes situation, there needs to be one officer in overall command of the investigation with the authority to direct the course of the investigation in all the police areas affected."

Byford's words were to have a huge impact on Hector Clark's career and the investigation into the deaths of Susan, Caroline and Sarah. When the Midlands Triangle murders occurred, leaving a number of s police forces stumped, Hector Clark was exactly what the probe needed. The choice of officer, Byford said, "is obviously of vital importance… The person appointed requires not only the professional competence which will inspire confidence in those who work for him but the charisma which will ensure loyalty to him and his policies." Procedural changes were afoot. Their implementation would make or break this investigation.

Long before the concept of a Family Liaison Officer was invented, Clark was ever conscious that crimes needed solving not for the sake of professional kudos or pride, but for the families of victims, whose lives had often been obliterated. Clark was determined to keep these families in the loop, to update them when possible and visit them regularly and in person. He went to visit Caroline's parents, both as a means of allowing them to ask questions and so that they might get to know him. He wanted them to have complete faith in what the police were doing, first to find their child and then to catch her killer.

Clark understood that achieving a successful outcome in any case required not just diligence, doggedness and intelligence – it also required the active participation of victims' families. Painful as it was for them, he knew that they needed to trust him. With this trust came the willingness to think deeply about what had happened and to confide in the officers assigned to their case. Families needed, too, a direct line of communication with those responsible for hunting a killer: without it, co-operation would falter.

The press was deeply invested in the stories, and any friction between the police and the families would, of course, be reported on, while also proving a distraction. Clark knew that the families of missing children in particular, and especially those abducted while they were out alone, would pick at their guilt like a wound. It was vital that officers understood this and made every effort to communicate effectively with them, "if for no other reason than to give them one less thing to worry about".[23] The years between Susan, Caroline and Sarah's murders were directed solely towards tracking this nameless, faceless killer: a predator who was unlikely to have commenced his crime spree with the abduction of Susan Maxwell, and who had likely been committing similar offences for some years. Who knew, Clark wondered, how many similar cases might also be linked to this man?

To catch a predator, Clark knew, it was vital to get to the start of the story, to build from the ground upward. At this stage, as his teams pored over witness statements and sightings, spoke to families and re-visited crime scenes over and over again, they had no such starting point. It was as though they had sat down in the midst of a twisty, plot-heavy thriller and been unable to catch up. They were in a roomful of doors, behind which lay innocence or guilt, but they had no way of establishing which was which.

Their man was invisible, it seemed. He might strike again at any moment. All they knew was that he was likely to do so in the northern counties before leaving his victim somewhere in the Midlands. It wasn't enough; they needed more. He made sure to leave little to no trace of himself or his crimes behind. How was that possible? Not a scrap of clothing, not a shoe print, not a tyre mark. And he struck in such quiet, remote places – summer lanes with nobody around to notice him, or stormy streets where people pulled their hoods down low, hid under their umbrellas, failed to spot the darkness in their midst.

But he was becoming careless. Perhaps, in his youth, the bodies of his victims had simply never been found, had never been dumped so shamelessly onto public roadsides. Maybe he had gone to great lengths to cover his tracks. His evasion from justice had only emboldened him. One does not wake up and decide, that day and for the first time, to commit a crime against a child – especially such a risky and vicious one – and leave evidence of that crime behind. The risk of capture should feel far too great. And that told Clark, however much he was loath to admit it, that their man was both cunning and arrogant, intelligent and confident. Easy to miss, perhaps. Hiding in plain sight.

"The reality of the position we were in," said Clark, "was that, over a period of seven years, three children had been abducted and murdered and despite a massive inquiry involving hundreds of people and millions of pounds we were absolutely clueless as to who was responsible."

On the afternoon Tom Wood – Deputy Chief Constable of Lothian and Borders Police – heard about the arrest in Stow, he sat back in his chair, his brow furrowed, then cleared. He had worked closely with Clark over the years, as the seasons changed, and still they had been unable to trace the children's killers.

He examined the case notes from the Caroline Hogg inquiry, and once again pulled the handwritten police report from Stow – 30th July 1990 – toward him. The child's father was one of their own, a man who'd spotted the similarity in the sketch artist's drawing, all the while confronting the person who'd tried to kidnap his child. That drawing had been dispersed far and wide throughout Scotland, while the original was placed in Caroline's file. He stared at the picture, at the eyes, the shape of the face, the hair. He forced himself to wipe his mind clean, to look at the image objectively, to take his time. Several minutes passed in silence. No. There was no doubt. Mackey had been right.

"That's got to be him," he whispered to himself. "Gotcha."

They had their man.

Now they just needed to prove it.

HAPPY TO TRAVEL

By chance, David Herkes, the retired postman, had borne witness to an abduction that would change the course of Clark's investigation forever. Clark himself understood that crime is often solved not necessarily by police, but by civilians: a witness who simply happened to be in the right place at the right time.

On the Monday following the attempted abduction, Clark arrived before 8am at the Selkirk police station where the perpetrator was being held prior to his appearance in court. The single-storey office was a quiet, non-descript sort of place – not one accustomed to the sort of serious criminal who now sat, watchful and waiting, in a cell usually reserved for drunk drivers and those accused of disrupting the peace after a heavy session at the local.

Clark and Watt watched the man as he sat on the bed, the point furthest from the door. His hair was badly in need of a wash, his clothes were old and threadbare and a strong smell of body odour emanated from him. Was this a general lack of hygiene, or the scent of fear?

"How are you doing?" Clark asked, looking closely at the man, who muttered a few indistinct words in response.

237

He was softly spoken, barely raising his head, avoiding eye contact.

"Are you comfortable? Have you had a cup of tea?"

Waiting for a few moments more, Clark and Watt left the cell and went back to the main office. Later that morning the scruffy, softly-spoken man would appear in court charged – as Scots law dictated – with the crime of "plagium" or child theft. At that point, he was remanded in police custody for a week.

On 10th August, the man appeared once more – this time at the High Court in Edinburgh. He spoke only to confirm his name and address.

"7 Stanmore Hill, London," he said quietly. "Robert Black."

Black seemed aware that an early confession would elicit little further investigation: he would be charged and sent to prison for a fixed period of time, before being released once more. If it weren't for the fact that Black unwittingly chose a policeman's child on that warm summer's day, he may well have escaped with a minimal custodial sentence and a criminal record detailing the nature of his offence.

Instead, Constable Mackey had recognised him.

Parliament House, on Edinburgh's Royal Mile, was once the home of the Scottish government from 1532 until its union with England in 1707. It's an imposing building, all grey stone, pillars and carved frescoes. Edinburgh's Old Town is largely given over to coffee shops and tourist attractions these days, tartan bedecking the windows; few Edinburghers live here, on this short stretch between the old castle and the royal palace. The tiny, twisting alleys are labyrinthine, rising steeply before falling away as quickly. There's something disorientating about it, something that seems to deliberately hide itself away. The little alleys, or wynds, lead all the way to Parliament House.

Some of Scotland's highest-profile and most notorious cases have been heard here, in the court's heavy stone walls and under its high, arched ceilings. It's worth noting the difference between the Scots and English systems, the different processes of justice. In Scotland, a combination of the language used in court, the attire of the officers present and the way in which the charges are read out all give a sense of gravity. Without the electric lights buzzing and flickering overhead, or the steady hum of traffic and horns in the distance, you could almost believe a time machine had transported you back to some distant medieval trial.

Black entered the court between two officers dressed in white gloves and carrying truncheons which – once he was seated – they laid across their knees. It was intimidating, deliberately so. The dock was separated by a small wooden fence, and behind it, on the first row of bench seats, sat the press; it was never, Clark reported, as packed as it was that first day. It seemed that others besides Clark, his team and the investigators on the Stow case had suspicions about who exactly this man was.

The macebearer led the judge, Lord Ross, to the bench. Ross had served as Lord Chief Justice Clerk since 1985. He was a direct contrast to his predecessor, a man led by a strong Roman Catholic value system who was, according to one report, "all fire and brimstone". Lord Ross, the son of a solicitor from Dundee, was a keen gardener, gentle in manner but with a reputation for tough sentencing. In 1992, his views on capital punishment caused controversy when he claimed that certain crimes warranted the death penalty: the killing of policemen and prison officers, some acts of terrorism and multiple killings. Robert Black may or may not have known this. In any case, he was soon to find out.

Ordinarily, the knowledge that a perpetrator planned to enter a guilty verdict might have soothed the worries of a policeman like Clark. It would have been almost impossible for Black to enter any other plea on this occasion, and Lord Ross was likely to impose a lengthy sentence. However, given Clark and his team's suspicions, the hard work was still to come. While Black might confess to the attempted abduction of Ella, they were convinced the man sat before them was responsible for a host of other crimes, all of which had ended tragically. Across the country there were at least three families and likely many more who survived, rather than lived, through their remaining days.

Clark and his team were not the only ones to listen intently. Officers from the other forces – some English, some Scottish – sat in rapt attention as the charge was read:

"Robert Black, prisoner in the prison of Edinburgh, you are indicted at the instance of the Right Honourable, the Lord Fraser of Carmylie, Her Majesty's Advocate, and that the charge against you is that you did on July 14, 1990… abduct [redacted], aged six years, care of Lothian and Borders

Police… and there did assault her by seizing hold of her, lift her into the front of a motor van, push her under a seat, cover her with a coat and blanket, order her to be quiet, and convey her against her will in the said motor van…"

The charge continued in all its grim detail. Black had ordered the girl to be quiet, taken off her shoes and socks and tied her hands behind her back before assaulting her. The court sat in stunned silence. Lord Fraser of Carmylie QC rose then to explain the facts of the case. A psychiatrist who had examined Black, he said, considered him a serious danger to children and explained he was likely to remain so for an indefinite period of time. If the child, found frightened in the back of the van on that warm summer's day, had not been discovered within an hour, she would have suffocated.

Black's defence lawyer, Mr Kerrigan, had little with which to counter the horrific facts of his client's case. He described Black's actions as a momentary lapse of self-control, one to which Black had succumbed where previously he had resisted. Pornography, Kerrigan argued, had until that July day provided the defendant with the means to resist becoming a direct threat to children.

Lord Ross listened, considered and passed sentence, praising David Herkes – the alert and resourceful neighbour – as a life-saver.

"The abduction of this little girl was carried out with chilling, cold calculation. This was no 'rush of blood', as you have claimed. This is a very serious case, an horrific, appalling case, and there are few words appropriate to describe the disgust with which one listens to the details of this offence."

"I am bound," he said, directly to Black, "to be greatly influenced by the opinion expressed by the psychiatrist… the fact that you are a serious danger to children and are likely to remain one for an indefinite time to come. There are no means by which children can be protected other than by detaining you in custody. The sentence is one that makes sure you cannot be released until such time as it is safe to do so… You will go to prison for life…"

Clark hurried down to the court cells immediately after the trial, hoping to catch Black in the immediate aftermath of receiving a life term, to get the information he needed while the defendant reeled, as he digested the fact of his incarceration. He was to be disappointed: Black was unresponsive, and said barely a word.

Ray Wyre was a celebrated criminologist and the founder of the Gracewell Clinic, a dedicated residential treatment centre for sex offenders in Birmingham. Originally trained as a prison probation officer, he'd worked with Reggie Kray and several other notorious criminals. He was tasked with offering a second opinion on Black following the initial psychiatric report.

Wyre was unusual in his refusal to dismiss or turn away from society's worst offences and those who committed them. He believed firmly in the capacity for change, no matter how serious the crime. By providing a calm and uninterrupted space in which to discuss what had brought an individual to him, he was often able – with a high degree of accuracy – to identify other crimes an offender might have committed, and help them understand why they'd done so. It was this dual approach – one that was intended to help the families of cold-case murder victims, but also the offender themselves – which lent him a fearsome and highly respected reputation.

Wyre had been tasked by Black's defence team to provide this second opinion; in the event, he would spend 18 months interviewing the man. Wyre had worked for five years with category-A inmates at Albay prison, on the Isle of Wight, where he pioneered the work for which he became famous. "No one wanted me to do this…" he said. "They thought sex offenders were one-offs and wouldn't do it again; they didn't understand that it's a lifelong pattern of behaviour and that unless people go through therapy while in prison, they'll go straight out and resume where they left off." Wyre was often consulted in cases of major sexual crime.

In 1986, just three months after the terrible discovery of Sarah Harper's body, and before Black was arrested, police headquarters in Bradford became the site of the new Child Murder Bureau. This was an initiative designed to look cohesively at unsolved cases of child abduction and murder since 1973 – specifically of girls under 16. Perhaps historic crimes, previously thought unconnected, would help detectives in their quest to work backwards, to find the first victim.

The Bureau discovered that between 1973 and the end of July 1986, 18 female child abductions and murders – including those of Susan, Caroline and Sarah – had gone unsolved. Between that time and Black's capture in 1990, two men were found guilty of six of these. After the attempted abduction in Stow, police began drawing up lists of the remaining 12 victims, the forgotten, the case files nobody had opened properly for years.

Inside the Bureau on a cold, blustery winter's day, detectives arrived to find folders teetering on tables. Twelve cases, the paper now old, crinkled, the ink faded. Despite having taken place within the past 20 years, these crimes seemed to come from a different time entirely. Here the country's forces were now inputting data into machines that could forge connections it might take detectives months to uncover. The children in some of these files, all grainy black-and-white images and out-of-date haircuts, looked utterly at odds with the more modern, recognisable photographs they used for missing kids in the 1980s.

It was time to include or rule out the children in the case files. The detective on duty that day pulled the first towards him, opened it and began reading. His eyes scanned the facts, paused, moved on. Too urban. Too planned, too calculated. Probably taken on foot and via public transport. Unlikely, this one. Nothing fitted. He replaced the file, opened the next one.

Very quickly, he began to nod.

A 13-year-old on a bike. A quiet road in rural Norfolk, close to the motorway.

Black didn't formally acquire his driving licence until 1974, but he received a traffic conviction two years before this, suggesting he'd been operating vehicles before being legally allowed to do so. April, she was called. He pulled the next toward him. A younger girl this time. Same sort of boyish haircut, though. 1973, Scunthorpe. Never found. Both quick crimes, opportunistic.

The next file bore yet another detail that stood out: a lone bike, abandoned in a country lane, its back wheel spinning. He turned the page. He remembered the school photograph included here: the girl out delivering papers. There had been no signs of a struggle and no evidence left behind – the two schoolfriends walking just behind her in that five-minute window hadn't heard anything suspicious.

Ray Wyre was briefed on the situation and sat down with Black, attempting to coax him into revealing any concrete information relating to Ginny's disappearance. With the trial for Susan, Caroline and Sarah's murders fast approaching, Wyre knew his time was running out. But Black was still maintaining that the abduction attempt in Stow had been an isolated incident, the first of its kind. So Wyre asked him where he'd had the idea to abduct a child in the first place.

"Maybe…" said Black in response, "there was that paper girl that went missing. I don't know where she was missing, like, but it was all over the papers… She disappeared. She never turned up." When probed further, he offered the following: "He obviously persuaded her to get off her bike, or grabbed her off the bike, one of the two. Then got her into a vehicle and took her away." When asked why he'd drawn that conclusion, Black replied simply, "It seemed obvious to me."

The arrest of Robert Black drew an enormous amount of speculation in the press. The high-profile cases of Susan

Maxwell, Caroline Hogg and Sarah Harper – all unsolved, and all very similar in nature to the abduction of the child in Stow – led to inevitable parallels being drawn long before the police had managed to build even the smallest foundation of evidence against him. Clark and his officers had a long road ahead of them, and they'd no idea what they might uncover along the way. The possibilities seemed endless, grimly so.

A picture was emerging, but slowly, like a Polaroid gradually coming into focus. Police began the unenviable task of trying to place Black's movements in the summers of 1982, 1983 and 1986 – no mean feat before the widespread use of pagers or mobiles, CCTV and transactions via debit card rather than cash.

Detective Superintendent Andrew Watt had been placed in command along with a deputy, Roger Orr – they both reported to Hector Clark, but were attempting to fit the pieces of the jigsaw together when it came to Black's history and movements over the past eight years. For most people in the 1980s and early 1990s, traceability was barely a concern. One could move fairly undetected between jobs, flats, countries even, with little evidence of such movements – again, a symptom of the last days before computers and the data they could harvest became widespread.

However, Andrew and Roger discovered almost immediately that where Black's childhood and adolescence were concerned, there was ample evidence. He was extremely well-known to authorities in Scotland – from the very time of his birth he had been, in essence, a ward of the state. And each subsequent movement, from foster parents to children's homes to borstal and finally to London, had been documented in all its depraved detail.

What's more, detectives knew he was based in London, and it didn't take long to interview Black's landlords, the Raysons, as well as associates from his frequent visits to local pubs. Despite his love of sports as a boy and teenager, it did not appear that Black, now a grown man, much enjoyed the outdoor life – darts, listening to music and amassing an ever-growing collection of child pornography had been revealed as key interests, all of which were solitary, indoor activities. He spent the majority of his time alone, though occasionally attended family gatherings with the Raysons; clearly, whatever their feelings about Black, they did not feel threatened or intimidated by him, and the children had never reported inappropriate behaviour from Black of any kind.

But how, then, could they connect a strange, lonely man from London not only to Scotland, Leeds and Northumberland but to the Midlands as well? How did the darts player in Stamford Hill happen upon Caroline, Susan and Sarah? Perhaps, in Caroline's case, the proximity between Portobello and Musselburgh (where Black briefly attended school some 30 years prior to her abduction) suggested a geographic link. But what about the others? If Black's hobbies and interests did not take him out of the capital, all the way up to Scotland, then something else did.

When Robert Black first arrived in London, it's clear he started a series of jobs, but most quickly fell through. He took occasional work as a lifeguard; complaints were filed against him and he was summarily fired.

It wasn't until 1976 that Black found a job that suited exactly what he wanted to do. He was 29 now, with a string of stop-start homes, run-ins with police, constant movement and at least three jobs from which he had previously been fired. Now with the Raysons' help and support he seemed to have found stable work at last. As turning points go, this could have been one for Robert Black – a moment of transformation, a fresh start. He could have put the past behind him and moved on.

Instead, he took a job as a delivery driver.

"It's not particularly hard, as jobs go," said the manager of Poster, Dispatch and Storage, lighting a cigarette. "Long hours, which some of the boys don't like." He eyed the man sitting before him, who remained perfectly still, listening. Outside, the roar of London traffic was gearing up for the day; it was a little after eight in the morning.

"I don't mind that," he said eventually. "Could use the money."

"You'd be away from home a fair bit on the longer runs," said the older man, exhaling smoke through his nostrils. "Again, some of them prefer to keep it local. We can offer week-on, week-off shifts for the heavy-duty distances if you'd prefer."

Black shook his head. "No need. What's the farthest you deliver?"

"We go all over. There are depots at pretty much every English city you can think of. Off to the east, near Norwich. South West, Devon, Cornwall, that sort of thing. Up to Scotland a fair bit too. Might be nice for you if you've family back up there."

Black blinked, surprised by the reference to his accent. "No family. But I'll go where I'm sent, whatever you want. Happy to travel."

"Some of the drop-off points are pretty remote. The boys can tell you about the back roads, the cut-throughs off the motorways. Make sure you're not sitting in too much traffic."

Black smiled. "Sounds fine. Thanks."

In 1986, Black was briefly fired from PDS after a series of small car accidents; feeling they were having to pay out too much in insurance, the firm let him go. But when the company was bought out by two employees, he was reinstated. Black was seen as a hard worker, one who never seemed to mind going the extra mile – quite literally.

Where some of his colleagues struggled to fit in the often days-long absences required for longer trips alongside their family life, this was no concern for Black. He willingly volunteered for extra shifts, and as a result was described in favourable terms by fellow employees. Most importantly, he was ever-willing to take the London to Scotland route – likely the least popular due to its length – and would combine the trips with stopovers in the Midlands, where John Rayson, his landlords' son, was now living with his own family. To get there, Black would use the A444 road, the one that passed Twycross.

Andrew Watt and Roger Orr had a mammoth task ahead of them. For the 15 years prior to his arrest in Stow, Black had crossed the length and breadth of the UK delivering posters to be displayed on billboards. PDS ran a large fleet of van drivers who would leave the capital for a whole host of different depots ready to receive the posters for advertising campaigns, the majority just outside large cities. Few of them required staff to be present, and the drivers would ordinarily drop the deliveries into large boxes outside the depots.

There were therefore few time constraints, and drivers were at liberty to stop off at will en route, spending an afternoon here or there as the fancy took them. As long as the posters were delivered within a certain time frame there was no issue; it was a far cry from the fast-paced, frenetic series of drop-offs an average delivery driver will face today.

Watt and Orr were also labouring with the task of gathering together a dossier of times that Black had bought petrol in or near to where the abductions took place. Poster, Dispatch and Storage held accounts with several oil companies which allowed their drivers to buy fuel without cash; instead, employees were given dedicated credit-card slips.

The companies handed over some seven million microfiche slips for police to sift through – transactions which had occurred at several premises across the country between 1982 and 1986. They spent weeks sifting through these, looking for Black's signature and cross-referencing the dates and times of purchase. It was this painstaking work that persuaded the Crown that there was a case to be answered. The CPS clearly felt there was a fair amount of evidence against Black. The problem, as Hector Clark knew all too well, was that all of it was circumstantial.

The day of judgement meant more than professional pride – much more. Hector Clark felt he owed it to the families. He had never promised to catch the man he felt was responsible for their children's deaths, but he might as well have done. The best part of 10 years had been consumed with hunting their invisible quarry.

Black was already expected to remain in prison for life – or at least until such time as he no longer posed a risk to children, or indeed to anyone else. In some ways the work of the police was already done: he was, at the very least, off the streets, off the highways and byways of the UK. The cases of Susan Maxwell, Caroline Hogg and Sarah Harper all bore his trademark, but there was nothing concrete, not a single piece of evidence relating to any of the murders that could be linked to Black.

This was a major issue. How could police hope to convince a jury, beyond all reasonable doubt, that their suspect was responsible for the murders? Whether he was found guilty or not, he would remain in prison for some time to come. But this wasn't the point. A not-guilty verdict would shatter the girls' grieving families, especially since police had maintained for so long that they had their man.

We know, now, that every contact leaves a trace. It's just that the trace needs searching for. Black had – apparently

– left no sign of himself at the abduction sites and, while children's clothing had been found in the van in Stow, none of it proved a match to Susan, Caroline or Sarah.

But why would it? Police knew that Black had used many different vans over the 15 years he had worked for PDS. One or more of those vehicles would contain the clues they required, but the evidence was impossible to locate without firm proof. Even if it could be determined that Black had indeed driven certain vans on certain days, those days were now long enough ago to cast potential doubt. If other drivers had used the vans before or after Black – which they doubtless had – then fibre evidence, hair or other DNA material could easily be dismissed. None of the vehicles used by Black in his abductions were owned by him personally until the late 1980s.

As the date of the trial edged closer, the prosecution and defence had engaged legal teams to work on the case. John Milford was a QC from Tyneside with an excellent reputation; Toby Hedgeworth and Roger Cooper were the prosecution's juniors.

Newcastle's Crown Court was ordinarily used for crimes of this magnitude, but on this occasion the old Moot Hall courthouse had been reopened specially for the case against Black. This, the city's original courts of justice, stood beside the keep of the long-demolished wooden castle built on the banks of the Tyne on the orders of William the Conqueror: the castle which had given the city of Newcastle its name, though by this point it was a millennium old.

The number one court was to be the location for a case that could last, potential jurors were warned, some three months. It was an imposing space, lined with oak and wooden pillars. The panels gave the odd appearance of windows in this claustrophobic, intimidating place. The judge's seat was placed high above other benches, and the defendant's dock was in the middle. All around this square contraption stood a row of sharp black spikes. A steep flight of steps in painted white brick led down to the cells below.

It was 13 April 1994, almost four years since his arrest. Black arrived, as he would do for each subsequent day of the trial, in an unescorted police minibus at exactly half past nine in the morning, his head covered in a blanket. The media, as anticipated, had flocked to catch a glimpse of the man. Fifty reporters sat on the benches waiting, their eyes glued to the stairs from which – like some terrible, mythical beast – the accused would appear.

Their first sight of him would likely have surprised them. Here was an underwhelming figure in a tired grey suit – borrowed, since his own clothes had long since rotted away in evidence bags – with a short beard and moustache, both greying, and a blue legal notebook he brought with him each day but was never seen to use.

"Robert Black," asked the clerk, "please stand." Black did so. The clerk read through the charges against him and asked him to respond to each, which Black did. "How do you plead?"

"Not guilty."

Not guilty to the kidnap and murder of Susan and Sarah. Not guilty to preventing their lawful burial. Not guilty of Caroline's "unlawful imprisonment" (so-called since her kidnap, which occurred in Scotland, was beyond the English courts' jurisdiction), her murder or the prevention of her burial.

Juries can, of course, prove instrumental in the winning or losing of a case like this. This jury comprised six men and six women, most of whom were under the age of 30, with two looking to be under 20. Whether or not that would help or hinder the case remained to be seen.

Jackie Harper, Sarah's mother, was the only parent present. "When I was told they'd arrested Robert Black for Sarah's death," she told Ray Wyre, "I think I felt relieved. Firstly because then I could put a face and a name to him, and I could stop suspecting people that were talking to me, wondering 'Am I talking to my daughter's murderer?' And secondly, relieved because he would not be able to do it again."

The four years since her child's death had done little to diminish the pain or make it easier: "I knew I had to go to the trial. I had to know what he'd done. I never saw my daughter's body... that's very difficult to come to terms with, not seeing her. I don't know what he did – I've a vague outline, but I don't know what he did. I can only imagine – and the reality can't be any worse than the imagining."

Jackie was accompanied by a detective from the West Yorkshire police to help her throughout. Mr and Mrs Maxwell and Mr and Mrs Hogg had decided against sitting through the days and weeks in court, staring at the man who – they were sure – had taken their children away.

The judge was Justice Macpherson, a stalwart of the profession who'd overseen some of the country's most high-profile cases. He'd been a high court judge for 11 years by this point, following a predictable career for the hereditary chief of a Scottish clan, from Oxford to the Bar. He was remembered by colleagues for his warmth and charisma, and Clark recalled this courtesy in action when it came to the jury at Black's trial, whom Macpherson took pains to guide and whom he regularly thanked throughout.

Just three years after Black's trial, Macpherson was appointed head of the inquiry into the murder of Stephen Lawrence, a report which saw the first coinage of the phrase "institutional racism" and through which Macpherson made over 70 recommendations – including the establishment of police accountability, the advent of the Independent Police Complaints Commission and the capacity for retrial in any legal case when new evidence was discovered – essentially the abolishment of so-called "double jeopardy".

Mr Milford, for the prosecution, began proceedings on that spring day. He outlined the case against Black and described the circumstances of each case for some five hours. "It would be too easy to dwell on the suffering," Milford said, "but we have to put that to one side, along with all our natural emotions, and consider only this: it is proved by the evidence that this defendant, Robert Black, abducted and killed them."

The court sat in silence as Milford continued. "These three offences were so unusual, points of similarity so numerous and peculiar, that you can, members of the jury, safely conclude that they were all the work of one man."

He explained that petrol receipts and eye-witness statements could place Black at the abduction sites and the sites at which the bodies were discovered. Black's proximity to these sites on the dates in question was proof, surely. Any other possible explanation was "an affront to common sense". Black's lack of involvement in the crimes would be "the coincidence to end all coincidences".

James Fraser, a member of the Lothian and Borders Police forensic laboratory, had conducted painstaking work on more than 300 items seized from Black's Stamford Hill bedsit. He'd been tasked with linking these with items recovered from the van.

"And did you," asked the defence, "find any forensic link between our client and the items so carefully examined... I believe some 1,800 microscopic comparisons?"

Fraser admitted the team had not. Milford rose to re-examine his witness, pointing out that the time between each of the murders, and the fact that Black's latest van had been acquired as late as 1986, would make any direct forensic link impossible to find.

By the trial's second day, statements, forensic reports and circumstantial evidence were offered. Witnesses described the white van, with its curtained back windows, parked waiting by the River Tweed when Susan was snatched off the street. "Black was known to sleep in the van," the prosecution argued, "and had hung material over the back windows."

When it came to Caroline's disappearance, it was striking how many of the witnesses – even after 11 years – could remember the day so vividly. The event had been burned onto their collective memories, though barely any were above the age of 10 on that summer's day in 1983.

It fell to junior counsel to read the mountains-worth of facts, poster delivery times and locations or fuel-purchase receipts. Ronald Thwaites QC, the counsel for defence, did attempt to cross-examine some of the witnesses on minor quibbles: times logged in record books when Black made his deliveries, for instance, or petrol receipts. He also questioned the accuracy of their memory.

But the painstaking, agonising work of Hector Clark's teams was indisputable.

Pathologists were also called, those whose grim task it had been to perform autopsies on the victims: they presented their findings to court. Neither Caroline nor Susan's bodies revealed signs of sexual assault or injury, and they were almost certainly dead by the time their bodies were disposed of. Sarah, it was concluded, was still alive when she entered the freezing River Trent, though likely unconscious. She had been the victim of a serious sexual assault, described starkly as "simply terrible" by the pathologist. All three were likely strangled.

Black made no comment throughout these readings or statements. He sat, relaxed, his legs outstretched, and seemed simply to watch, to drink it all in. His facial expression remained calm, almost tranquil. Perhaps he had detached himself, mentally, from the events described; perhaps he did not recognise himself in the explanations and witness reports being slowly accumulated, like so much rubbish at a dumping ground. With each fresh detail, each receipt or character report he sat, nonplussed.

That is, until the Raysons took the stand on the 11th day.

Eddie and Katherine Rayson had been the closest things Black ever had to a family; he had lived with them for 20 years and considered them close friends. Yet here they were, appearing as witnesses for the Crown. Devastatingly for him, the Raysons' two sons Raymond and John would provide some of the most damning evidence of all. Raymond reported the discovery of a "suitcase-full" of child pornography in Black's Stamford Hill bedroom, along with girls' swimwear.

John, the brother who had relocated to the Midlands, described his old lodger's frequent visits to their new houses in Twycross, and provided a video clip from his twin children's birthday party. Black can clearly be seen filming the young guests. He explained that he and Black had often shared a drink in Twycross, while another family friend stated Black had been present at John's house on the weekend of 18th July 1993: the weekend that Caroline Hogg's body was found in the lay-by minutes down the motorway.

It was with John that Black had found the deepest and most lasting connection. He had married Angeline Compton in 1971, a local woman, and for seven years the newlyweds lived a short drive from Eddie and Katherine in north-west

London. John and Angeline then moved to Shenstone, a small village in Staffordshire.

The bodies of Susan, Caroline and Sarah were all discovered close to the village of Donisthorpe, to where John and his wife had since moved. The location of a murderer's victims can provide police with as much of a clue as the nature of the murder itself. It was highly unusual to find a case where victims had been transported such a great distance from their abduction sites; not since records began after the Second World War had such a situation arisen. Donisthorpe was a regular stopping point for Black on his frequent visits to John and Angeline Rayson: though a small and rural village, it lies extremely close to a network of busy A roads. The Raysons lived at The Hawthorns, a smart house off the Acresford Road, which runs into the A444.

Black was observed fidgeting as the Raysons gave their evidence. John explained that Black would visit himself, Angeline and their twins, Christopher and James, at least 10 times a year. Within minutes Black had begun to look down at his feet, and shortly afterward his head hung low, almost touching his knees.

If ever there was a time at which Black might have changed his plea, it was today. At the close of proceedings, his legal team spent considerable time with him – presumably urging exactly this course of action – but Black remained steadfast. He would continue to fight the charges laid against him.

There was so much, so very many corroborating reports and stories, testimonies and eyewitnesses, a mountain of geographical evidence and – crucially – the holy trinity of policing: means, motive and opportunity. It was clear that Black's motivation – indeed the motivation of a lifetime – was indecent attacks on children. He was provided with the means, however unwittingly, through a line of work that actively encouraged a great deal of travel. often to remote spots outside of urban areas. This same line of work provided the vehicles he would use to transport his victims after he had struck, and it was in these that he would pause, shamelessly, to toss out their lifeless bodies.

And yet the defence was preparing its pitch, sharpening its claws. At various stages it presented motions to ban the reporting of certain interview snippets, of comments made by Black while not under police caution or at the police station in Selkirk immediately after his arrest in Stow. These were met with varying degrees of success. Meanwhile the police, and eventually Hector Clark himself, were called to present portions of the evidence gathered.

Officers took the stand to describe the painstaking work that had been completed over the past decade and more. Some 20 tonnes of material evidence had been gathered, examined and assessed. It is incredible to think that these crimes, so opportunistic and random, and completed within the space of seconds, could have resulted in such a mountain of incriminating evidence.

Fellow officers were cross-examined on details related to other suspects in the children's abductions, vehicles unaccounted for or never eliminated from enquiries. Clark was the prosecution's last witness, called on the 13th day of the trial.

Hector Clark's experience lent additional gravitas to his already weighty words. He stated that in 39 years – almost four decades – of policing, he had never come across any unsolved cases of child murder which involved the transportation of the victim's body over such lengthy north-to-south distances He conceded that Black's name had not been logged in the Holmes database because he was not a known sex offender. His molestation of a previous landlord's daughter occurred in 1976: too far back to have been registered.

Just as he was about to leave the witness box, Justice Macpherson asked a final question:

"Do you, Inspector Clark, know of any criminal investigation larger or more thorough than this?"

Clark paused.

"I know of none bigger," he replied. "But I am not the right person to comment on the thoroughness of what we have done."[24]By this point it was the May Day bank holiday, and the jury had been asked not to return until the following Wednesday. The papers satisfied themselves with the ever more grisly discoveries 200 miles south west, in Gloucestershire, where for the past months human remains had been discovered in the growing case against Fred and Rosemary West. Just three days before Black's trial began, the body of West's first wife, Catherine Costello, was discovered in a field. While the Black trial paused briefly and the defence rolled up its sleeves, Rose West was charged with three of the same murders as her husband. And on the day the jury returned, Wednesday 4th May, a body believed to be that of Fred's daughter, Charmaine West, was discovered. She had last been seen in 1971, at the age of eight.

The defence's strategy, when it came, was unsurprising. Ronald Thwaites first attacked the police, who for eight years prior to Black's arrest in Stow had proved themselves unable – despite all the tools in their arsenal – to catch the person responsible. The investigation, he said, "reeked of failure, disappointment and frustration".

Mr Thwaites rose to outline his position. He explained that Black was currently serving life for the crime committed in Stow. He described Black's "lifelong" interest in children, particularly girls, and that he was undoubtedly a danger to children. However, and this was key, he urged the jury to examine the facts. "This case has been determined using one incidence of abduction, which he admitted, as a substitute for evidence in all the other cases. Without it, there is no direct evidence against him."

While Robert Black was certainly a paedophile – there was no question about this – he was not, Thwaites argued, a murderer.

"Where is the jury," he asked, "that will acquit a pervert of multiple murder?"

While there was a great deal of animosity felt towards Black, there was nothing concrete to suggest he had been involved in any of the murders for which he stood accused.

"The police have become exhausted in not finding anyone; the public are clamouring for a result. What good are you if you can't catch a child killer? Is he their salvation, or a convenient expendable scapegoat?"

He went on to describe the terrible strain of detectives across the four counties involved. It had been 12 years since Susan's murder by this point, 11 since Caroline's and seven since Sarah's. These three children ought now to be in their late teens or early 20s, forging lives of their own, experiencing the world. Instead they were dead, and while this was a terrible tragedy, it was important to consider the toll these cases had taken on police desperate to charge someone – the implication being "anyone" – with these awful crimes. Thwaites posited the theory that detectives were exhausted, broken by the case and keen to find their man – whoever, at this stage, that might be, and whether or not he was innocent.

His next technique was the calling of witnesses. Many witnesses. Witnesses who had seen other vehicles, other suspects. There was not, the defence maintained, so much as a hair's worth of evidence to implicate Black in any of the murders for which he was being tried. The police had nothing but guesswork, coincidence – and for that, there could be no verdict reached but "not guilty".

It must have been a frightening time for Clark and his team. Despite the masses of evidence compiled, checked and cross-referenced, there was an element of truth to what the defence maintained. It was a slim possibility, but a possibility nonetheless.

Had they managed to sway the jurors into spotting the similarities, the none-too-easily-dismissed hallmarks of a killer who had been caught in the act of kidnap not three years before? Did the fact Black had been in the areas where Susan, Caroline and Sarah went missing count for nothing – would the jury feel persuaded by Thwaites' argument?

Perhaps the six men and six women would examine the distance between Black's drop-off point in Morley and Sarah Harper's home and decide it was mere happenstance. Perhaps the witnesses' memories had faded, or they'd been coerced by a prosecution team desperate to see a resolution for these families. No one had any way of predicting what might happen next.

It was May: sunny, bright and full of the hope and excitement of summer. The school holidays were just a few short weeks away – a time Black was known to have prowled. On the 16th, just over a month after the trial had commenced, Justice Macpherson began his summing-up to the jury.

Across the course of that day, he outlined the evidence and brought attention to various aspects for consideration. He explained the importance of remaining impartial, and that neither distaste felt for Black or his known record of sexual offences, nor the incident in Stow, was to sway their judgement. It was 3pm when he sent them home and asked that they begin their deliberations the following day, Tuesday 17th. After the first day they were sent to a local hotel, ready to begin again on Wednesday. Macpherson advised that they were welcome to return a verdict if 10 or more jurors could agree on the charges. More waiting began. The Moot Hall at Newcastle was surrounded by press and photographers, reporters and police standing smoking, looking at their watches, pacing across the forecourts, staring longingly at a café but worrying the call to return could come at any moment.

On the third day, the jury once again retired to consider. The sun beat down and everyone prepared for another long day's wait. Neck-ties were loosened, heads scratched, yawns stifled. But not long after 11.15, just an hour or so after they'd convened, the jury were ready.

Here were Sarah's mother, and Caroline and Susan's parents. They sat, staring down from the public gallery, as one by one the 12 people in whom they must now rely filed back into the court.

"The verdict will be heard in silence," said Justice Macpherson. "Have you," he asked, addressing the jury, "reached verdicts on all 10 charges faced by the accused?"

The foreman announced that they had. The first charge related to Susan Claire Maxwell. This was it. It was impossible to believe Black had committed this crime but not the others. If they were sending him down for this, then they were sending him down for everything.

"And what is your verdict?"

"Guilty, your honour."

Black was handed 10 life sentences. He appeared nonplussed by the verdict, perhaps expecting it. As he was led down the steps and away to the start of this fresh sentence, he turned back once to address the watching constables and detectives.

"Tremendous," he said, the hint of a Scottish accent still audible in his voice. "Well done boys."

Part Five

Never Again

WHAT HAVE WE LEARNT?

The trial marked an ending of sorts, but it also spurred detectives on. What they wanted now was information relating to other unsolved crimes. At a police conference in Newcastle in July, officers sat down to assess what they knew and what could be assumed.

The Child Murder Bureau – with its list of unsolved abductions and murders bearing similarities to Black's known modus operandi – was re-examined. Two years later, in December 2009, detectives from Ulster visited Black – who was at the time incarcerated at Wakefield Prison, West Yorkshire – to inform him he would be charged with another crime.

The Cardy family – Andrew, his wife Patricia, Mark, their eldest, Jennifer, Philip and Victoria, who was a baby – lived in Ballinderry, County Antrim, around 20 miles west of Belfast. On 12th August 1981, nine-year-old Jennifer was planning to visit her friend Louise, who lived 20 minutes away by bicycle. She'd be home, she said, in time to watch the children's TV programme *Jackanory*, which aired at 4.30pm. It was just a fortnight after the landmark marriage of Prince Charles and Princess Diana, when the country had been gripped by wedding fever and everywhere you looked, merchandise and memorabilia abounded. Jennifer and Louise had watched the fairy-tale event together, glued to the events as they unfolded on screen.

When Jennifer set off, she was wearing a white T-shirt with strawberries on it, a red watch which she'd asked her mother to wind to the correct time, a white cardigan and red trousers. Jennifer did not arrive back home for her TV programme, and the police were called.

The all-too-familiar narrative unfolded like a hideous dream sequence: the cries of friends and family as they shouted the missing child's name, the police officers scouring roads and fields and ditches. And then the discovery of Jennifer's bright-red bicycle, a present from her father after she'd outgrown her previous one. It had been tossed over the hedge a mile from her home on the route she would have cycled, and was covered over with leaves and branches. It was found with its stand down, suggesting Jennifer had stopped her bike.

On Tuesday 18th, six days later, two duck-hunters spotted something red in the shallow waters of McKee's Dam, a large pond popular with anglers outside Hillsborough, 15 miles south east of Crumlin, where Jennifer lived. The pond lies at the edge of a dual carriageway, in a lay-by connecting the busy arterial road between Belfast and Dublin. It was and remains a frequent stopping-point for long-distance drivers.

Jennifer's father, Andy Cardy, made the grim journey to the mortuary to identify his daughter's body, which was found in just six inches of water surrounded by the long weeds of the dam. She was still wearing her white cardigan and red trousers. Pathologists noted signs of sexual abuse on Jennifer's body; her red watch had stopped at 5.40pm.

It is not clear why Jennifer's abduction and murder were not linked to Sarah Harper's case five years later. Perhaps the destruction of all evidence played its part: in 1992, as investigators were busy preparing the case against Black with regards to Susan, Caroline and Sarah, a Provisional IRA bomb destroyed the forensic laboratory in Belfast where Jennifer's clothing was being held. Any fragment of evidence was now gone.

It wasn't until a 2005 cold-case review that Black was even questioned about what would appear, on the surface, to be his first murder. As police painstakingly reviewed the files, petrol receipts revealed Black had been in Northern Ireland on the day of Jennifer's disappearance.

The families of Susan Maxwell, Caroline Hogg and Sarah Harper were all contacted. Robert Black, the man serving multiple life sentences for the murders of their children, was once more about to come under the spotlight.

On 22nd January 2010, Black appeared at Northern Ireland's Lisburn Magistrates Court charged with Jennifer's murder. Later the following year, at Armagh Crown Court, forensic pathologist Dr Nathaniel Cary explained to the jury that Jennifer's case could be directly compared with that of Sarah Harper's, claiming that the circumstances of their deaths were "remarkably similar... These cases are very rare. So if a rare thing has similar features, that's an important point."

Just as before, prosecutors relied on such similarities. The lead in Jennifer's case, Toby Hedworth, drew the jury's attention to the fact that Black was delivering posters in the area close to where Jennifer was abducted, and that she, like the others, was pre-pubescent, wearing white socks, out alone during the school holidays, placed in water like Sarah Harper, transported away in a car or van, and was likely kidnapped with a sexual motive in mind, whether or not that particular crime had taken place. Hedworth claimed that Jennifer's murder "bears Robert Black's signature". The jury returned a guilty verdict. Black was convicted of Jennifer's abduction and murder on 27th October 2011.

A further life sentence, a further terrible charge to add to a list investigators had only managed to scratch the surface of.

"You subjected a vulnerable child to unpardonable terror and took away her life," said the judge, in his summing up. "By the manner of that loss, you also wounded for ever a family that treasured that child. It was a wicked deed."

It's 2016, a chilly January morning. The man was old now, a year shy of his 70th birthday. How much the world had changed around him as he remained the same. It had been over two decades since his incarceration for the children's murders. Now he sat on the slim bed at Maghaberry Prison. The name in translation conjures images of its surroundings: *Maigh gCabraí*, the plain of poor land, was a small village best known for its farming and limestone quarries. Hard, immovable stone and land meant for tilling.

None of the men here share a room, not one of the 700 –
many of whom are Republican paramilitaries. In 2012, the New
IRA had murdered one of the prison guards as he drove to work.
It's a high-security facility, this, housing the long-term sentenced.
Just a few months before, the prison had been branded unsafe,
unstable, in dire need of change. The Chief Inspectorate had
declared its "state of crisis" in a damning report. Here, prisoners
were locked inside their cells for long stretches. In 2014, one such
inmate – at high risk of self-harm and with severe mental-health
issues – successfully gouged out both his own eyes before guards
intervened. Maghaberry has seen it all, and worse.

Robert Black suffered a stroke in 1996, just two years into his
sentence for the murders of Susan, Caroline and Sarah. His left
side was weakened considerably as a result, and the intervening
years had been none too kind, a combination of heart attacks,
angina and deep-vein thrombosis. A lifelong smoker, he had also
been diagnosed with diabetes the previous year; a ticking time
bomb of high cholesterol and blood pressure, he had been urged
to stop smoking but claimed he was not interested in doing so.

On the morning of 12th January, a decade after his
stroke, Black was preparing to move cells. He packed up his
few belongings and made to leave.

The familiar shooting pain travelling down his left arm
was the first sign of an attack; his collapse was the second.
Within an instant, he was lying dead on the floor of his cell.

His body was taken to Belfast for cremation at Roselawn
Cemetery. Ordinarily, the crematorium shut its doors after
the final service at 4pm. On 29th January, the lights were

switched off as usual and all was silent inside the chapel. What no one knew was that an additional, secret service was scheduled for 5pm, and 20 minutes before the hour the lights flickered dimly back into life.

Black's body arrived in a black Ford Mondeo car, its seats folded down to allow space for the wooden coffin, which was placed onto a trolley and wheeled inside the chapel. There were no flowers and no mourners, despite the prison's attempts to trace family members. Prisons are obligated to arrange a final service for those in their custody who die without family or friends to claim responsibility for funeral plans. In this case, authorities had attempted to keep plans away from the press: the outcry at any public money being spent would likely have been enormous.

The Maghaberry chaplain presided over the six-minute service, which included a passage from Psalm 90. No reference was made to Black's life or crimes. His coffin was swept into the furnace, his ashes later scattered at sea.

Black's death inevitably brought much pain to the families of his victims. For decades their grief had moved into a new dimension – from fresh, sharp wounds to the sort of scar that penetrates deep into the skin's tissue, the sort that will never heal. From time to time, they might run a tentative hand over its surface, testing its ability to spark memories, to recall torment. The sort that, occasionally – and in particular on days like this – seems to twinge and ache.

Life had changed so much since those days when their children were young. Would any of the girls recognise this strange new world? The quiet lanes of Cornhill-on-Tweed, the busy beaches at Portobello and the suburban warren of Morley could now be quickly viewed at the click of a button, the country mapped in pale white lines on computer screens. The ditches, lakes and cul de sacs which they roamed so desperately all those years ago appeared innocent, so anodyne when computerised. What would the girls think of iPhones and Facebook, driverless cars and devices that, when instructed, played music or news or recited a joke?

The year of Robert Black's death was, just like that of his birth, a momentous one. The UK was reeling in the wake of the Brexit vote when another vote – this time in the United States – brought still more unrest, uncertainty and discord. It was a year marked by unexpected celebrity deaths, like David Bowie and Prince, by the rapid spread of the Zika virus. The Queen celebrated her 90th birthday and polymer bank notes entered into circulation.

Detectives were unsure about how much, exactly, John Tate would digest the information they were approaching him with. He was an old man now, as so many involved with the early cases were. He was sick: very sick. It was impossible to spot the young, determined father who'd raced through the fields of Aylesbeare all those many years ago. His daughter would herself be in her 60s now, maybe even a grandmother. She'd have lived all those years and John would have been there to see them. Barely anybody remembered her now. But there, beside his bed, on the night stand, was the picture. The cheeky grin, the pixie haircut, the large front teeth only revealed by the breadth of the smile – one that reached her eyes.

The inquiry into his daughter's disappearance involved some 3,000 lines of investigation, 2,000 statements, ponds and wells dredged, tracker dogs combing the landscape and volunteers walking for miles across fields, through hedges and ditches. Rewards were offered and, when the technology became available, infrared aerial photos were also used. Thousands of people had once been involved and now, all these years later, most were gone or had forgotten.

Black was interviewed in connection with Genette's case in 1998, but denied involvement. Back in 2002, one of Ginny's jumpers was found to contain tiny fragments of her DNA – clothing preserved lovingly by her mother and which might, one day, prove instrumental in the identification of any human remains discovered. A year later, John and Sheila both stated their conviction that their child was no longer alive.

So much time had passed. It was unlikely anyone remembered. The world had changed: modern-day 13-year-olds were frantically clicking through Snapchat and Instagram, completing their homework online, begging their parents for hoverboards or virtual-reality headsets.

John knew his daughter was dead. What he didn't know was that police were about to pay him a visit, that now – 50 years after the crime – they had a possible solution.

He could barely lift his head as two officers knocked on the door of the quiet bedroom where he spent the majority of his days. A man and a woman entered, dressed in plain clothes.

"May we take a seat?" asked the woman, waiting until John nodded to do so. They were young, these two, he thought.

Very young. How old had they been back then – when Ginny vanished? Were they even born?

The discussion was brief, to the point. The police had established a suspect in the disappearance of John's daughter.

"We've been reviewing the case file," said the man. His colleague pulled a photograph from her folder. She handed it to John.

John reached out and took the picture. He stared at the image of the man with the thick, round glasses and fading dark hair, the piercing blue eyes. For a few seconds there was silence.

"Do you recognise him?" asked the woman.

Although he had long since moved away, John's mind was never far from Aylesbeare. That bright sunny day. Violet's laughter coming down the stairs, pulling a scarf over her hair, ready for work. Tania and Ginny, later, sleepily eating toast in the kitchen. Ginny on the grass outside, humming quietly to herself. What had he missed? How many times had he been over and over those moments, chastising himself for not insisting Ginny join him as he drove Tania to the coach station? How often had he wished he'd never allowed her to do that paper round. It was, he felt, his fault.

Now, as his eyes roved over the face of the man in the picture, he forced his mind away from recollections of Ginny. He did not know this person, but could he have seen him?

"You asked me before," he said, slowly.

It was true. In 2005, Devon and Cornwall Police interviewed Black again, and had submitted a file to the Crown Prosecution Service. In 2008, the CPS decided there was insufficient evidence to charge Black. The investigators had hoped to tie Black to Ginny's disappearance. There wasn't enough.

"We know he killed Genette Tate and April Fabb," remarked a senior officer in the *Daily Express*, "and we believe that their bodies are buried somewhere in the Midlands Triangle." John had been kept abreast of all developments, waiting for the telephone call that never came.

"Was he there?" he asked slowly, annunciating each word as clearly as he could.

"We don't know. It does seem he could well have been in Exeter on the day Genette went missing."

"Ginny."

"Yes, I'm sorry. Ginny. He worked as a van driver, as you know. Drove all over the country. We've tried to locate receipts linking him to Exeter that day, but we've not been able to find anything."

John's brow creased. "But… why are you here, then? How do you know it's him?"

"We don't," said the man. "It could have been someone else, that's a possibility. But it's unlikely. A witness has claimed she recognised Black from newspaper photographs. She said he was watching her children while leaning on a red transit-style van at Exeter Airport. This was on the day Ginny went missing."

There was silence. The officer continued. "Again, as you know, this man abducted several other girls. Four that we know of, and in all probability more that we never will. He acted quickly. He did not plan his crimes. Ginny's case bears a striking similarity to the others this man was arrested, charged and convicted of."

"They were committed without forethought, it seems," said the woman. She looked sympathetically at John. "He knew the shortcuts and back routes, the roads no one else did. He knew how to cut across the country without detection. He was based in London and his few acquaintances had no idea what he was doing. He was known to stop and wait, park up or drive aimlessly around, looking for children on their own."

The pair waited, watching as John brought the photo up to his face, narrowing his eyes.

"I don't recognise him," he said, slowly. "I'm sure I'd have remembered if I'd seen him that day. The day she went missing, I mean."

"This will be very difficult to process, Mr Tate," said the man. "But this man's later crimes – the ones he was arrested and found guilty of – resulted in murder," said the man. "One child was saved in the nick of time. The others were left on roadsides for anyone to discover."

John stared back at him, his face expressionless. "I know my daughter is dead, detective," he said finally. "What I would like to know is who killed her, and how, and why."

The man sitting by the side of John Tate's bed leant forward. "I understand that. Our hunch is that if he was responsible for Ginny's kidnapping, the fact his later victims were discovered doesn't necessarily exclude him. He was younger, back in the 1970s. Unsure of himself, possibly horrified by what he was doing. Wanting to hide it away, ensure it was never uncovered."

"Well, if that's the case, he was successful," said John shortly. The detectives were taken aback by the sudden strength of his words. "What you're saying is, he could have taken her away anywhere at all. Miles from Aylesbeare, from Exeter, from Devon. Possibly out of the country completely." His mind leapt back to the evenings spent on Withen Lane, combing the hedgerows for clues. The biting winds and snow blanketing the little bridge; the springtime sun as it melted the ice and he scrabbled on the ground, looking for anything the weather might have dislodged.

"Yes, that's right," said the woman.

They were silent for a moment.

"What makes you think he took Ginny?" John asked, finally.

"His other victims were of a similar age," said the man. "They were out alone at the time, but not routinely, by any stretch. We knew they must have been abducted very quickly, because we never had witnesses confirming a sighting of the children afterwards. And that suggests a vehicle. Ginny was only out of sight of the other girls for a matter of minutes before they found her bike. It would have been impossible to lead her away without a car or van. And he," pointing to the photograph, "was driving long before he had his licence. He was also involved in a number of incidents as a teenager and younger man, all of them related to young girls. He moved around continuously."

"There's nothing concrete to prove his guilt at this stage," said the woman, "but his original trial centred primarily on the vast coincidences between the crimes he was accused of. And then, in 1990, he was caught mid-abduction in Scotland, and the pieces began to fall into place. We planned to charge him."

"His name," she said gently, after a pause, "was Robert Black."

John's voice, when it came, was shaky and soft. Miles from the broad, wide-vowelled manner of speech that reporters of the 1970s would have remembered.

"Was?"

"This man recently died in prison," said the male detective. "We were just five weeks away from submitting a new file to prosecutors. This file would have linked Robert Black directly to Ginny's murder."

Meanwhile, at the Devon and Cornwall Police headquarters in Exeter, some 20,000 index cards remain, filed away. If Genette Tate's bike remains in police storage – and of that there's no guarantee, since storage space is ever at a premium, and it costs – there are modern-day tools that could well shed fresh forensic light on the case. Techniques like superglue fuming are ideal for locating prints on metal: the bike, for example, would be placed in a fuming chamber along with a bowl of precious metal and cyanoacrylate, or superglue. As both are heated and evaporate, they form a molecular bond which coats the item and sticks to grease secretions such as those made by fingerprints. Once the print is established it can then be run through databases, searching for a match. "The evidence is there," says Brian Hook. "The trick is finding it, establishing first what could be there, using critical thinking. I call it your best possible guesstimate. The question needs to be 'what might I find and where might I find it?'"

Perhaps – with the use of Holmes and other digital tools – the answer to this 50-year mystery will be investigated again one day. Perhaps there was some way of tracing Black back to Aylesbeare, speeding towards the village – a young man, the mother and daughter had said, with dark hair. After the files were submitted to the CPS, Detective Superintendent Paul Burgan commented that "early indications" suggested Black would indeed have been charged with Ginny's murder. It seemed the catalyst for reopening Ginny's case was the upheld conviction for Jennifer Cardy's murder, which "enabled us to use Black's unique offending and bad character evidence to connect him with this offence".

Black's crimes were far-flung, seemingly random, opportunistic. Parents would have been forgiven for assuming nowhere was safe after the well-publicised murders of Susan, Caroline and Sarah. But though the geography of the offences seemed to cover so much ground, it was precisely this – ultimately – that led to his prosecution.

Terry Green, who was manager for the FBI's Vicap division, noted that "geography is important for a whole lot of reasons." He explained that recent research revealed "many serial killers are compulsive drivers. Between crimes, they like to have days out, cruising around, 'window shopping' for victims. It helps them develop comfort zones – places they feel they could act out their fantasies and get away with their crimes."

Clearly, Black had ample opportunity to do exactly this. His work not only enabled but necessitated long journeys which – should he choose to take them – would see him driving through remote country lanes, cut-throughs and snickets, shortcuts unknown to the average day-tripper. "Some offenders we've spoken to said," commented Mr Green, "on occasion, they just drove aimlessly for hundreds of miles because it was something to do, then a possible target would catch their eye and waken their fantasy."

Perpetrators of serious crime are often categorised as being either "marauders" or "commuters", depending on whether they travel away from home or stay within a certain boundary during the execution of their crimes. Geo-profiling as a method of criminal tracking was introduced by Kim Rosso, a Canadian criminologist who has studied the patterns of serious crime in relation to an offender's home. His methods analyse the locations of connected, series-based crimes to establish where an offender might live, in turn enabling police to focus their investigations, to streamline. If a series of connected murders, arsons or rapes can be plotted on a map, "marauder" offenders will usually avoid a so-called buffer zone – the protective circle that's too close to home for an offender. Police can then focus their investigations there, or nearby.

Black was very much a commuter. There is little evidence to suggest he struck where he lived, in London. What united his crimes was their distance from home, and the relative proximity of the disposal sites to a known contact: the Raysons' son John.

Black's work enabled his crimes, but he was also canny
– he knew when children were most likely to be alone, out of
doors, free. The majority of the crimes attributed to him, or
of which he's suspected, took place in the long, lazy summer
months of the school holidays. Taking a child off a London
street was simply too risky, but the quiet backstreets of villages and hamlets around the rest of the country – places from
which he could abscond quickly, with all his knowledge of the
road network – provided a cloak to hide under.

It appears Black was in Exeter on the day of Ginny's disappearance. He was certainly driving a car, even if he hadn't yet
passed his test, at the time of April's. He was convicted of
Jennifer Cardy's death, which bore striking similarities both
to Sarah Harper's murder and to Ginny and April's: girls
alone or on bicycles.

And Black was, by all accounts, in Enniskillen, just half
an hour by car from Ballyshannon, dropping off billboard
posters around the time of Mary Boyle's disappearance from
County Donegal. Just a year before Mary vanished, Black
visited the village of Annagry, in western Donegal, before
delivering his posters just over the border in Northern Ireland.
He would return every year until around 1979; while there,
witnesses reported that he would park his van overnight in a
number of local pubs' car parks, drink at the bar and strike up
conversations. In 1978, he was reported to have followed two
separate children, urging them to come closer to the car on
the pretext of asking for directions; he drove off quickly when
realising that one of them, who had long hair, was a boy.

Several witnesses, including Mary's own twin sister, reported seeing a white van on the remote country lane near the Gallagher farmhouse on the day Mary went missing. Another witness came forward to report seeing a man in a van driving quickly away from the area; he looked, they said, like a priest – though not the sort you'd want to visit. Years later it was discovered that Black owned a high-necked black sweatshirt with white piping around the collar.

It is all, of course, circumstantial. Circumstantial enough that no charges were ever brought against Black in relation to April, Christine, Mary or Ginny's disappearances – and then, once their suspect had died, the ability to secure justice for the girls' families died with him.

But there are almost certainly others, other victims whose cases will likely never be resolved. Suzanne Lawrence was 14 when she disappeared from her home in north-east London, just an hour's drive from Black's rented room, at the height of the summer of 1979.

The high-profile case of Katrice Lee, the British toddler who disappeared in November 1981 from Germany, is another possible link. Katrice's family were stationed at British Army bases along the River Rhine, and the child went missing from a supermarket at a time when Black was known to be travelling in Germany, often to these camps, to deliver posters for alcohol and cigarette companies. In fact, Paderborn, where Katrice and her family lived, lies directly on Black's former delivery route on the German highway 33.

In 1985, a year before Sarah Harper's murder, a German girl called Silke Garden disappeared on her way to the dentist in the town of Detmold. Her body was found in a stream and she had been sexually assaulted; Black was making a delivery of posters to a British Army base nearby that same day.

Two years later, a 10-year-old French girl, Virginie Demas, was abducted from Neuilly-sur-Marne, a suburb to the east of Paris; Black was known to have made deliveries in Paris that day. Virginie was found dead in an orchard 22 miles away from the site of her abduction. In almost identical circumstances and in the same year, another French child was abducted from the Parisian suburb of Malakoff; she was found murdered just two hours later. Hemma Davy-Greedharry was 10 years old in May 1987; Black was known to travel along the same road where she was later discovered in Chatillon. And again, that same summer, just a month later in June, seven-year-old Perrine Vigneron was abducted. Her decomposed body was found in a field 20 miles away around three weeks later.

On the day Perrine's body was discovered, nine-year-old Sabine Dumont was taken from Bièvres on her way to buy a tube of white paint from a local shop. Her body was found the next day. In 2011, French police named Black as their prime suspect in the case.

Two years after Sabine's murder, in 1989, 11-year-old Ramona Herling vanished on her way to a swimming pool in Bad Driburg, North Rhine-Westphalia, Germany. It's a 25-minute drive from Paderborn, where Katrice went missing, to Bad Driburg.

Robert Black never confessed to any of his crimes except when caught red-handed in Stow, and his prison sentence was delivered according to the murders police felt confident charging him for. As with Dennis Nilsen, who was convicted of six counts of murder despite being known to have carried out at least 12, the true number of children whose lives were cut short by Black is almost certainly far, far higher. It's not enough to know that the man suspected of murdering a child is incarcerated for attacks against other children – never to be released. That all-important day in court was an opportunity for some closure denied to many families, most of whom will remain anonymous, quietly nursing their grief.

It is impossible to over-estimate the impact of losing a child, especially when their death occurred in violent circumstances. For the parents of all children described in this story, the pain is complicated further when there is no body to bury, no resting place to visit. Memories of their children are tinged forever by the manner of their deaths, the torture of their final hours in what must have seemed a cruel and painful world.

Winnie Johnson was the mother of Keith Bennett, the only victim of the Moors Murderers Ian Brady and Myra Hindley whose body was never recovered. For years, Winnie begged Brady to reveal the location of her son's body and, despite occasional glimmers of hope that he might do so, Brady allowed Winnie to die in 2012 without that most sought-after resolution. In an interview before her death, she described the suffering she had endured.

"A lost child is something that destroys part of you at the time and the rest of you slowly," she said. "It can and does drive you mad."

LOOKING AHEAD

It's impossible in a case like Robert Black's to find the first confirmed victim of abduction and or murder, the "victim zero". "There will have been an escalation," says Brian Hook. "Multiple abduction attempts, undoubtedly."

What is highly likely is that the "thrill" associated with Black's crimes became harder to achieve as time went on. Where once an abduction, assault and murder might have been enough, his later crimes proved the need for public recognition, for attention, for the swell of fury that accompanied the discovery of his victims' bodies. As much as anything else, it was outrage that propelled him forward – outrage and confidence. A lifetime's offending had seen minimal repercussions for his increasingly serious crimes: at every chance of rehabilitation, Black either could not or would not take the opportunity.

It's probable that if the 22-year-old Robert Black was responsible for April Fabb's disappearance, he made efforts to conceal this fact. The incredible amount of similarity between the circumstances of her disappearance and the other missing girls are too numerous to ignore. But if April was his first murder victim, the act itself may have frightened him enough to ensure evidence was never discovered. Perhaps, by the early 1980s, when Jennifer, Susan, Caroline and Sarah were murdered, he had grown careless or needed the additional thrill of leaving something behind for police to find.

Having Black in prison for so long before his death may have brought a degree of closure to the Harpers, Hoggs, Maxwells and Cardys. His links to cases like April's, Christine's, Mary's and Ginny's were assumed, but there wasn't enough to go on, none of the all-important "new and compelling evidence" required. The bodies of his earlier potential victims have never been recovered, and it is doubly difficult to bring a conviction for historic murder without concrete physical evidence or firm proof that the person in question is indeed dead.

It isn't the families alone who suffer in such circumstances. As we speak, Brian Hook sits looking at a facial reconstruction bust of an unnamed "Jane Doe". The woman was found in 2002, Brian retired four years later, and, in 2007, the unknown body was buried. The bust was presented to him by colleagues on his retirement. "We never found out her identity," he says. "But whenever we'd all met up in London, we'd raise a glass to her. We called her Lily. We'd sit there and ask ourselves what we'd missed, what we didn't do." The ripples of unsolved cases continue to be felt by those who set out with determination, those who worked day and night to bring some form of resolution. It's important to remember the officers, detectives and superintendents who, despite their best efforts, were hampered by time, by resources, by a lack of so much that we take for granted today.

In 2010, the government decided to disband the Forensic Science Service. It was a controversial decision taken, as so many are, with resources in mind. And it was one that failed to garner the press attention that other such cuts – such as those to the police, or the NHS – might attract.

Forensics by definition involves specific, time-consuming and, to the lay person, scientifically abstract work – it isn't easily understandable or accessible, and so its dissolution fails to grab much attention. With operating losses at some £2million a month, it was a decision taken with money in mind. Lab equipment in itself is extraordinarily expensive, and if private companies could offer the same quality control for a fraction of the price, it was agreed that a taxpayer-funded service should be wound down to make way for independent firms. Now, the FSS archives are all that remain for the later review of cold cases: these files, microscope slides, fibre and DNA samples are retained in case the private sector can later pick up the contracts to examine the evidence.

Dr Sara Payne, the mother of murdered schoolgirl Sarah, spoke out against the closure of these services – without them, she said, her daughter's killer would be a free man. Along with some of the country's leading forensic experts she warned "that the UK's justice system would take a backward step if the service closed". As Sara correctly pointed out, 90% of most current sex-offender cases rely on forensic services to bring a resolution. Without this service, many perpetrators of other crimes detailed in this book would never see justice served.

There was no way of knowing, back in the 1970s, that the key to almost all criminal cases lies in microscopic fragments, in fibres, tiny details left at the scene of the crime. April and Ginny's bikes were both discovered, as was Jennifer Cardy's. If Black had picked them up, tossing them over the hedges or pulling them to a stop, crucial evidence proving his guilt beyond reasonable doubt would have remained long enough for crime-scene investigators to search for, locate and mark it. Nowadays, most people who discover a crime know not to disturb the scene. In Ginny's case, it is unlikely her friend would have picked up her bike and ridden it home, potentially disturbing any prints left behind, any small pieces of clothing caught in the spokes or in the basket.

"He couldn't have got away with it today," says Brian. "The Police National Database is amalgamated with other databases, and it shares intelligence. We had it in place when Soham happened, but it wasn't being used correctly: you can lead the horse to water, but you can't make the bloody thing drink. We now have intelligence-sharing and organisations external to the police force, like the Police National Improvement Agency. We started to sing off the same song-sheet, and there was at last a sense of interoperability. Things are different now, we'd like to think."

While Black was coming to the end of his spree, the world was changing fast. In 1989, Tim Berners-Lee launched his plans for the World Wide Web, an online hosting platform for websites and pages, and he later developed a brand new digital language called HTML. By 1991, this first web page had become available. Lines of communication lit up around the world. It was as seismic as the invention of the printing press, as the Industrial Revolution, as radio and television and space flight. The internet as we know it today was born, and with it came both great potential and great risk.

Over the years, people realised its power. Now, police could remove the boxes stored in cold, quiet rooms and take a fresh look at the evidence, the reports, the handwritten notes – and they could input them, feed them into a machine that made connections, suggested routes of inquiry, threw up comparisons that a human mind – exhausted from another long nightshift or from a rumbling stomach, an argument with a spouse or bad news from a friend – might inadvertently overlook.

What Berners-Lee had provided police with, whether he anticipated this or not, was speed and efficiency. But he also paved the way for others – the armchair detectives – to do the same. Famous cases were and still are pored over on forums dedicated to crime, and the click of a smartphone can redirect a user to fresh information, a suddenly remembered fact from a long-silent witness, or enable them to make links investigators might not have pursued. Web-sleuths comb images on Google Earth, searching for clues and often finding them – an unexplored tract of land, a grainy image of a person standing in an open doorway. Instead of a dedicated team working in closely guarded police stations, social media and online communities have enabled anybody to investigate a crime, should they choose to.

Of course, there were now also dark, hidden places online that facilitated the sorts of material that people like Black favour. Policing and legislating for these took time initially, because those utilising the web's shadowy corners always seemed 10 steps ahead; comparing a pre- and post-internet age in terms of crime is impossible. They're totally different landscapes.

One might be forgiven for assuming men like Black simply don't exist anymore – the sort who opportunistically abduct children from the street – when in reality they're just finding new ways to exist. Suddenly, forums began to appear where predators just like Black validated their own fantasies among other "like-minded" people. It became apparent that the web had connected everyone, not just those with good intentions. And while the law caught up, killers slipped through the cracks.

But systems like Holmes enabled forces around the country to speak to each other, literally and metaphorically – to connect the dots in a way that, before, would have required meandering telephone conversations, painfully slow written reports posted and perhaps lost along the way, handwritten cards where a misspelled word or a smudge could allow a killer to remain on the loose for another day.

There are many what-ifs. If the bicycles belonging to April Fabb, Genette Tate and Jennifer Cardy had been processed for DNA examination today, the results could have been logged and compared.

Years later, DNA profiling sites like Ancestry and 23andme enable users to upload their genetic profiles online and discover more about their own heritage, find long-lost relatives and even detect a person's susceptibility to certain diseases.

In 2018, the so-called Golden State Killer – a man suspected of over 50 rapes and 13 murders between 1974 and 1986 in California – was arrested using just such techniques. Police had the killer's DNA from multiple scenes of crime, and submitted it to a variety of online testing sites; from this, they were able to match his profile to other publicly available profiles and find a familial match. Once police had a list of users whose DNA shared characteristics with the killer's, they cross-referenced family trees, looking for physical characteristics as reported by witnesses, as well as age, employment and other relevant factors – all of which ultimately led to the capture of Joseph DeAngelo.

Imagine investigators like Hector Clark knowing that somewhere, at any time, an unsuspecting member of the public might submit a swab sample to a lab. It could be on the other side of the world, it could be next door, but that swab could hold the key to a cold case. If Black's DNA remained on Jennifer's bike, and if it this had been logged digitally, a familial DNA match could well prove his guilt beyond reasonable doubt in a matter of seconds. And if the same could be done for Ginny and April, those families too would finally have the closure they so long fought to achieve.

When Robert Black began attacking children, the very notion of the internet was decades away. The country, indeed the world, was quite literally disconnected. If crimes were reported, they were often local rather than national, and faded quickly: the old adage that today's news is tomorrow's fish and chips. Black was aided, inadvertently, by this lack of connectivity.

It would have been near-impossible for police to link a missing girl in Norfolk with another in Ireland 11 years later, or spot the similar patterns these abductions shared. Black was further aided by the comparative lack of CCTV, the lack of a national database, the lack of digitisation. Nowadays it's possible to track a person's movements from A to B and back again in a matter of minutes. There is more power in the tiny computers we hold in our hands – that we rely on for so much – than most of us realise. But not so for Black. There was everything to help him and nothing to stop him.

In 1993, just three years after he was arrested in Stow, CCTV footage captured three young boys walking out of a shopping centre in Merseyside. While Robert Thompson walked ahead, Jon Venables was holding the hand of a smaller child, Jamie Bulger, who was found murdered two days later on a railway line in Liverpool. When a member of the public recognised the two older children, who were both 10 at the time, she contacted police and the boys were arrested.

CCTV was the primary lead for police who had initially – and quite understandably – believed they were hunting a lone paedophile. It remains one of the most notorious crimes in British history, but it also ushered in public acceptance of the necessity of round-the-clock surveillance. Less than a year after the crime, Liverpool city centre's CCTV system was launched – something that might well have been met with disapproval were it not for the dreadful Bulger case.

There will be countless girls – women now, and some of them very old – who knowingly or unwittingly came close to the fates met by those in this story. Those who, due to a change of schedule, a rainy day or a flat bicycle tyre decided not to go out on the day Black was driving towards or returning from a delivery. Some will be all too aware of how close they came.

In April 1988, 15-year-old Teresa Thornhill was walking home with her boyfriend Andrew in Nottingham. At just four foot eleven, Teresa was 15, but looked younger. When she and Andrew said goodbye at the end of the street, she spotted a blue Transit van stopping ahead of her. The driver climbed out, lifted the bonnet of the van and asked Teresa if she knew how to fix engines. Startled, she said no and walked on briskly. Suddenly, she was grabbed from behind; the man was dragging her backwards, towards the door of the van.

She fought him, grabbing and biting him until Andrew, hearing the commotion, arrived and the man ran back to the driver's seat of the van, started the ignition and roared off. When the terrified teenagers arrived at Teresa's house, the police were immediately called. Teresa remembered the man as overweight, balding, between 40 and 50 and around five foot seven.

In 1987 Black had been reinstated by PDS, but new management required all drivers to be self-employed. They'd have their own vans and work on a freelance basis: by 1988, Black's regular van was a blue Ford Transit. On the weekend of Teresa's attempted abduction, Black was the only driver who used his petrol-agency card to buy fuel.

He dropped off posters advertising Trebor mints and Stones bitter and continued on to Nottingham. Detectives would later find security footage from a branch of NatWest which showed the exact make and model of the van described by Teresa and Andy, though the focus cut off the registration plate. Teresa's evidence – as collected by Roger Orr for Hector Clark – was to prove instrumental in Black's 1994 trial. Her recall of Black's general appearance was almost photographic, while specific details – tinted glasses found at Black's London flat, for instance – helped link him conclusively to her attempted kidnapping.

Once convicted, Black confessed to Ray Wyre, the criminologist whose interviews with the killer were to prove so enlightening. "I don't know what possessed me in Nottingham," he said, "like, you know, in broad daylight in the middle of the day... She was with a boy. I thought she looked about 11 or 12."

In Teresa's case, the knowledge of what could have happened was, and likely remains, all too real. There will be countless others who, for a whole host of reasons, only mildly suspect how close they might have come to the same fates as Susan Maxwell, Caroline Hogg, Sarah Harper or Jennifer Cardy. To the decades-long mysteries of the disappeared like April, Christine, Mary, Ginny.

There will be girls, women now, and, particularly those living in the areas most affected by these cases, who will recall the proximity of that danger. These are women who went on to have full, rich lives, the ones who grew up to become adults, experiencing the world, only dimly suspecting how close they might have come.

Girls from Metton in Norfolk, or Scunthorpe, or Donegal or Aylesbeare, who remember the speeding van that slowed to a crawl beside them, who recall the screech of tyres as it took off quickly. Their relief at the sight of a waving parent round the corner, a dog, a sibling or a group of friends.

Perhaps the danger paused, watched, and moved on. It brushed past stealthily. Maybe they felt its cold hand on their arm for the briefest of moments, a barely registered shiver, a collision avoided at the very last minute. The threat slunk off, unseen and invisible, leaving a fleeting rush of confused and unfocused fear, a shudder of distaste and a quick glance around. The girls turned, scanned for the source of that odd, unsettling feeling, shrugged.

Then forgot all about it.

BIBLIOGRAPHY

Bilton, Michael, *Wicked Beyond Belief: The Hunt for the Yorkshire Ripper*, HarperPress, 2012

Cardy, Patricia, *There Came a Day: A Child's Murder, A Mother's Survival*, 10Publishing, 2021

Clark, Hector with David Johnson, *Fear the Stranger: The Murders of Susan Maxwell, Caroline Hogg and Sarah Harper*, Mainstream Publishing, 1994Clark, Chris and Robert Giles, *The Face of Evil: The True Story of Serial Killer, Robert Black*, John Blake Publishing Ltd, 2017

Clarke, Chris and Tim Tate, *Yorkshire Ripper – The Secret Murders: The True Story of Serial Killer Peter Sutcliffe's Reign of Terror*, John Blake Publishing, 2015

Cottle, Simon, *The Racist Murder of Stephen Lawrence: Media Performance and Public Transformation*, Praeger, 2004

Cummins, Barry, *Without Trace, Gill & Macmillan Ltd*, 2010

Cummins, Barry, *Missing: Ireland's Disappeared, Gill & Macmillan*, 2010

Gallop, Angela, *When The Dogs Don't Bark: A Forensic Scientist's Search for the Truth*, Hodder & Stoughton, 2019

Greer, Chris, *Sex Crime and the Media: Sex Offending and the Press in a Divided Society*, Greer, Chris (2003) Sex Crime and the Media: Sex Offending and the Press in a Divided Society. Willan, pp. 1-229.

Kinder, Gary, *The Other Side of Murder, Atlantic Monthly Press, 1999*

Payne, Sara, *Letters to Sarah: a child lost forever, a mother's grief and a love that will never die, John Blake Publishing, 2017* Morson, Maurice, *The Lost Years: The Story of April Fabb, Redbridge Books of Norwich, 2012*

Shepherd, Dr Richard, *Unnatural Causes: The Life and Many Deaths of Britain's Top Forensic Pathologist, Michael Joseph, 2018*

Wells, Kevin, *Goodbye, Dearest Holly, Hodder Paperbacks, 2005*

Wyre, Ray and Tim Tate, *The Murder of Childhood, Penguin, 1995*

ACKNOWLEDGEMENTS

With thanks also to the British Newspaper Archive www. britishnewspaperarchive.co.uk

Thanks to David & Charles Ltd for permission to reproduce quotes from John Tate's book Genette Is Missing. Thank you also to Jo Sollis for her editorial guidance and to Brian Hook for his invaluable help.

Many thanks to Flora, Anisa, Hannah, Laura and Lottie for their endless support, George and Helen for their patience and kindness, Marco for his humour and love, and Chris and Debbie – for everything.

ENDNOTES

1   Dr Angela Gallop, *When the Dogs Don't Bark,* Hodder & Stoughton (21 Feb. 2019)

2   *Crime investigation: physical evidence and the police laboratory.* New York: Interscience Publishers, Inc., 1953.

3   Mark Kermode, *The Observer*, 31 May 2015

4   John Tate, *Genette is Missing*, David & Charles, first edition (19 Aug. 1979)

5   Ibid.

6   Ibid.

7   Ibid.

8   Ibid.

9   Ibid.

10 Ibid.

11 Kevin Wells, *Goodbye Dearest Holly*, Hodder Paperbacks, UK edition (26 Sep. 2005)

12 Ibid.

13 John Tate, *Genette is Missing*, c.David & Charles, first edition (19 Aug. 1979)

14 Ibid.

15 Ibid.

16 Ibid.

17   Ibid.

18   Potts, Lauren (26 December 2016). "Patrick Warren and David Spencer: The mystery of the Milk Carton Kids". BBC News

19   www.openaccess.city.ac.uk/id/eprint/2013/1/2010%20-%20Sage%20 Handbook%20-%20News%20Media%20Criminology.pdf

20   www.gov.uk/government/publications/sir-lawrence-byford-report-in-to-the-police-handling-of-the-yorkshire-ripper-case

21   Pseudonym

22   Newcastle upon Tyne Crown Court

23   Hector Clark, *Fear the Stranger: The Murders of Susan Maxwell, Caroline Hogg and Sarah Harper*, Hector Clark with David Johnson, Mainstream Publishing, 1994

24   Ibid.